LEGENDS OF
1950s

Bert Bell

Commissioner De Benneville Bell was enshrined in the Pro Football Hall of Fame in 1963. Bell was a graduate of Pennsylvania and later became owner of the Philadelphia Eagles in 1933. He suffered heavy financial losses and was forced to sell the team in 1940. In 1941, Bell became co-owner of the Pittsburgh Steelers. Upon becoming the National Football League commissioner in 1946, Bert sold his co-ownership of the Steelers. As commissioner (1946–1959) he built and brought the National Football League to unprecedented heights. Bell was the commanding officer in the NFL's war with the AAFC. He also had the foresight to dictate policy regarding the use of a new media called television and how it would embellish the game of football. Bell also established strong antigambling controls within the NFL and recognized the NFL Players Association. He was born February 25, 1895, in Philadelphia, Pennsylvania, and died October 11, 1959, at age 64. He said, "On any given Sunday, any team can beat any other team."

On the front cover: Baltimore Colts quarterback Johnny Unitas is seen here. (Courtesy of the NFL.)

On the back cover: Coach Vince Lombardi is in the locker room with three future hall of famers, No. 51 Jim Ringo, No. 15 Bart Starr, and No. 31 Jim Taylor. (Courtesy of the NFL.)

Cover background: Seen here are colleagues of Johnny Unitas. (Courtesy of the NFL.)

LEGENDS OF THE HALL

1950S

Kristine Setting Clark

ARCADIA
PUBLISHING

This book is dedicated to those extraordinary men who played in professional football's greatest era, the fabulous 1950s—a time when football players were football players and the grass was still real.

CONTENTS

ACKNOWLEDGMENTS

I would like to express my appreciation to Pro Football Hall of Fame member Ron Mix and his wife, Patti, for allowing me to reproduce their hall of fame sports art cards—platinum edition; to Gary Gertzog of the NFL legal department; Bob Carroll and the Pro Football Writers of America; the Pro Football Hall of Fame; Upton Bell; Martin Jacobs; Lane Nomellini; Sherill Jones and Dottie Donovan for their personal photographs; and finally Steve Sabol and Kathy Davis of NFL Films for their continued support in making my books a reality.

I would also like to thank the archive, media, and public relations employees of the NFL teams who were so helpful in supplying photographs for this book: Baltimore Colts, Chicago Bears, Chicago Cardinals, Cleveland Browns, Detroit Lions, Green Bay Packers, New York Giants, Philadelphia Eagles, Pittsburgh Steelers, San Francisco 49ers, Los Angeles Rams, and Washington Redskins.

On a personal note, to Robert Schnitzer, photographer, graphic artist, and San Francisco educator, whose hours of hard work and dedication made this book possible.

FOREWORD

Football has been my whole life. My teachers used to say, "Y if you don't quit looking out the window at those guys kicking the football you'll never amount to anything." Maybe they were right, but football was always my number one interest.

I grew up in Marshall, Texas, where I watched my brother play both junior high and high school football. At the end of his senior year he was awarded a football scholarship to play at Tulane University.

Although he was seven years my senior, I was extremely influenced by his love for the game. Because of him, football became the love of my life since I was in the first grade.

My own football career began in 1938. I played junior high school ball for three years for the Marshall Jr. Mavericks. I went on to play four years in high school for the Marshall Mavericks. From 1944 through 1947 I played football for Louisiana State University (LSU).

Of course I had played before the T-formation had come into existence. I was a single-wing tailback both in high school and college. In high school I had made All-District tailback for two consecutive years. In college I played tailback in my first year (1944) and then we switched to the new T-formation where I made All-Southeastern Conference in 1946 and 1947.

I refer to this time as the "golden era" of college football. Many of the players were returning from military service. Some of these players had already played football two years prior to being inducted and then continued to play football while still in the service. Many were older than I. College football was truly at its best.

The rules of the collegiate game were different back then. For example it was illegal to send information from the sidelines to the quarterback. You couldn't hand signal or send in a substitute to tell you what to do because you could only substitute one time per quarter. If you went out of the ball game in the first quarter you couldn't come back in until the second quarter. So there was no way to get communication to the quarterback. If you even tried to communicate from the sideline it was a 15-yard penalty for illegal coaching.

The quarterback was also the signal caller with no help from the sidelines. Whenever a substitute came into the huddle the referee would stick his head inside of the huddle with the substitute to be sure that he didn't talk to the quarterback. The substitute couldn't talk to the quarterback until after the first play. That was the rule and you couldn't call time out. Let's say it was fourth down and two, and you wanted to go for it. If you looked over at the sidelines and one of the coaches moved his foot forward, as if to tell you to kick it, your team would be hit with a penalty and it would cost you 15 yards.

At LSU the coach found a way of communicating with the quarterback without getting caught.

Whenever our team would a call time out, the water boy would bring to the huddle 10 or 12 half pints of water. One of the pints would have a different colored cap on it. I knew that one was for the quarterback. When I would pull the cap off it would say something like "punt on two," or maybe "29 sweep x cross" (a pass pattern). The information came from my coach who, of course, was on the sidelines.

One time in 1945 we were playing Texas A&M. It was fourth down with a yard to go. We only had 30 seconds left in the ball game. Obviously, we needed to make a first down.

I called time and our water boy came out with the water bottles. I opened mine (the one with the green cap) and it said "punt." I thought, "This can't be right. Why would we punt the ball with only 30 seconds left in the ball game when we were behind six to nothing? This is stupid!"

But being the disciplined player that I was, I got in the huddle and said, "Quick kick." Right then all 10 ball players went crazy.

They said, "Are you dumb? What are you talking about—quick kickin' the ball? The score is six to nothing!"

"I don't care," I said. "That's what we are supposed to do. We are kicking it!" I said.

We kicked the ball and it went out of bounds on the two-yard line. Texas A&M got the ball and tried to run an off tackle play hoping to kill the clock. They ended up fumbling. We recovered the ball and called time out. There were nine seconds to go in the game. I threw the winning touchdown pass and we beat them seven to six.

After the game I found out why the coach called for a quick kick.

What had happened was that the coach had forgotten to take off the cap and change the play. The play that I had read was from the third quarter when he sent in the play that said punt. I thought it was the wrong thing to do but following orders, I punted.

The next day the newspapers had written that it was the most brilliant call that any 18-year-old quarterback had ever made in the history of LSU. I was a hero. If they had only known.

In 1948, I was drafted out of LSU and sent to the pros.

At that time, there were two leagues in professional football. The AAFC (All-American Football Conference) and the NFL. While I was at LSU, I didn't even know that there were two separate leagues.

As it turned out, I was the AAFC Cleveland Browns' first draft choice and I was also the NFL Detroit Lions' first draft choice.

Cleveland contacted me after the last game of the season (Tulane) and told me I was their first draft choice. They took me to New York for their championship game and I stayed at the Waldorf Astoria. It was the first time I had been on an airplane. They wined and dined me. I signed a contract with Cleveland.

Six months later before the season had started, Commissioner Bert Bell wanted to strengthen the league of the AAFC, so they took my contract and gave it to the Baltimore Colts, who were also part of the AAFC. I played my first three years with Baltimore before coming to San Francisco and playing with the 49ers.

Baltimore coach Cecil Isabel convinced me that I could win and that I was the best. He always kept telling me, "Y, don't pay attention to Frankie Albert or Otto Graham. You are the best!" He convinced me of that and I still believe it.

In 1950, the two leagues merged and the Baltimore franchise folded. The players from that team were redrafted. I was now San Francisco's first choice. I'm the only player in history to be the first draft choice of three teams—once with the Cleveland Browns, once with the Detroit Lions, and once with the 49ers.

There were many outstanding players in the 1950s. The 49ers had Hugh McElhenny, John Henry Johnson, and Joe Perry. Including myself, we are the only complete backfield in the hall of fame. We were known as the Million Dollar Backfield.

It was hard for me as a quarterback to choose who would get the ball because all three were runners and they all wanted to run the ball. I couldn't play favorites so I had to keep in mind who carried the ball and how many times they carried it. They were great players and we were a great offensive team in the 1950s, but we never won a championship. Our toughest opponents were the Detroit Lions and Los Angeles Rams.

Detroit had a great quarterback in Bobby Layne, great linebacker in Joe Schmidt, and great defensive back in Yale Lary. The Rams standouts were quarterback Norm "the Dutchman" Van Broklin, halfback Elroy "Crazylegs" Hirsch, and cornerback Dick "Night Train" Lane.

Other than having John Henry Johnson and Joe Perry on my team, there were few black players in the league. Cleveland had Marion Motley and Bill Willis. They were big stars. Other outstanding black players were George Taliaferro who played with New York, as did Buddy Young and Emlin Tunnell.

I played a total of 17 seasons in professional football—three seasons with the Baltimore Colts, 10 seasons with the San Francisco 49ers, and four seasons with the New York Giants.

In those days, the team only had two quarterbacks. So if you got hurt, you might get dumped, so you played hurt. If I could walk, I played.

I received a triple fractured cheekbone from Detroit's Jim David. I was running for a touchdown when he tackled me and his knee slammed into my face. I twice received a separated shoulder from 49er Ed Henke, and Baltimore's Eugene "Big Daddy" Lipscomb tore the cartilage in my chest. The cartilage tear was the toughest injury of all because every time I got hit, it was extremely painful. Most injuries can be taped, but you can't tape rib cartilage. That was the injury that led to the demise of my career.

I retired from the New York Giants in 1964. By then, many of the players that I had played with had either retired or were traded.

Being inducted into the Pro Football Hall of Fame in 1971 was my greatest thrill. All my children were there to witness me going into the hall. For any football player to be inducted and to be considered as one of the greatest football players of all time has to be the highlight and a memory that you will never forget.

As for the game of today, well, it has changed quite a bit. The rules have created that. The game is now wide open. A player can now use his hands when pass blocking. My right tackle and hall of fame colleague Bob St. Clair didn't have the luxury of using his hands to pass block. He wasn't supposed to, but he did it anyway. And he got away with it most of the time.

I don't think that the game has changed for the better. I don't like the free substitution rules where you can send in six, seven, or eight players at a time.

Sometimes, I don't even know who is in the game. Having four or five people coming in and out on every down can be really confusing. Today's fans don't get the opportunity to develop a favorite player. Players in the 1950s had distinctive and separate personalities. The fans knew them because they played every down.

I liked the game that was played in the 1950s much more than I like today's game. In the past we did our own thing and quarterbacks called their own plays with the help of their teammates on the field.

In today's game they have some guy in the press box with three or four assistants. They sit there with a battery of television monitors watching every down situation. They then send the play down to the coach who relays it to the quarterback and he repeats what the people upstairs said.

When the game is over can you say that the quarterback called a bad game? No, you can't, because he didn't make the call! The people upstairs did! Can the sportswriters say that the quarterback threw wildly today? Maybe he didn't because the guys weren't open and it really wasn't his fault, or maybe because the play selection was poor. The sportswriters criticize the players when they don't even know who is calling the plays. I don't like it but that's the system.

I enjoyed my era because I could be my own boss. I liked to do things my way because I knew what I could do well and not so well. I was a good outside passer because I could hit people outside. I could hit deep corners or deep sidelines—anything that was one on one.

Today you also have the benefit of the black athlete. We didn't have that benefit. Not very many schools in the south allowed blacks to go to college. We only had half the population to work with.

The camaraderie in the 1950s was the last of its kind. It was a continuation of the 1930s and 1940s. In the 1950s we did it (the 11 guys on offense and the 11 guys on defense)—not so much the coaches. Our coaches prepared us for the game but on game day the game was mostly turned over to the players.

Football in the 1950s was the final era before the big salaries, expansion teams, and the big money. I was so fortunate to have played in football's golden era—an era filled with so many great players. The good friends I had made through football are friends to this day. I wouldn't trade the time I played for any other era in professional football.

Y. A. Tittle
Pro Football Hall of Fame

INTRODUCTION

Legends of the Hall: 1950s captures a period of time when the sport really began to move forward into the new decade. America was now a mighty world power and playing football was for tough, rough, honest men who played solely for the love of the game.

These men were not only tough and rugged, they were young and fearless. Many of them had been forced to grow up in a hurry. They had just returned home from fighting a brutal war on distant, dangerous shores.

The 1950s was an era of crew cuts and Crazylegs, Hopalong, and Night Train, the hula hoop, and Alley Oop. These nicknames, like 1950s fads and fashions, became part of the American scene. But at the dawn of the decade, professional football was barely even on the map.

The NFL consisted of 12 teams in 11 cities with 33 players on each team. They played a 12 game schedule for most of the decade. A total of 72 games were played throughout the entire NFL season.

The game was about to make an impact on America's consciousness and for those just beginning to discover the NFL, it was love at first sight, thanks to a colorful collection of gridiron characters whose low salaries never dampened their high spirits. It was a time when $20,000 salaries were the exception and $6,000 salaries were the rule. It was the last pure football, played by a select few.

During the 1950s, professional football entered into its marriage with television. Thanks to television, the game was transported out of the backwaters of the American sports scene and thrust into the mainstream. But on-field pageantry and on-air highlight shows had yet to reach maturity.

With its unique way of capturing the spontaneity and immediacy of live events, television proved to be the perfect medium for professional football.

Aside from the fast action and hard hitting, television also highlighted the game's personalities. Men like Frank Gifford, Ollie Matson, Gino Marchetti, Bob St. Clair, Sam Huff, Chuck Bednarik, Art Donovan, Joe Schmidt, Marion Motley, Raymond Berry, Jim Brown, Lenny Moore, and Doak Walker were just a few of the larger-than-life heroes in a long-running, dramatic series that ran every Sunday.

The 1950s also produced some of the greatest quarterbacks ever to play the game. They were known as the glamour boys of the league—Sid Luckman, Otto Graham, Bob Waterfield, Norm Van Brocklin, Bobby Layne, Y. A. Tittle, Bart Starr, Charley Connerly, and Sammy Baugh.

The style of the era was typified by goofy gimmicks like the "hidden ball play" and "dipsy do," and by the kind of fast-paced spontaneity one might find in the slapstick comedy of television stars such as Milton Berle and Sid Caesar.

Pro football's popularity grew by leaps and bounds. Per game attendance increased in every year of the decade. Season ticket prices were $21 and individual game tickets were $4 and $5.

The 1958 championship game saw the Baltimore Colts beat the New York Giants in overtime. The game, long hailed as "the greatest game ever played" because of its impact on the sport, was televised nationally. An estimated 30 million viewers tuned in to see what would become "the game of the decade."

This championship game carried every element of football drama—great catches, unbelievable runs and goal line stands, eight fumbles, and eight quarterback sacks. There was even a cable break that cut off transmission for several minutes causing an emotional frenzy in millions of homes around the nation. It was 59 minutes of prelude setting the stage for an unforgettable finish—the first sudden-death game in football history.

The portrait gallery of greats established in the 1950s includes some of the most exciting athletes to have ever played the game. Of the 241 men enshrined in the Pro Football Hall of Fame, 70 players spent all or part of their playing careers in the 1950s.

In the NFL the decade of the 1950s began with Sammy Baugh throwing his last passes and marked the exit of pioneers such as Curly Lambeau and Steve Owen. It ended with the death of Bert Bell. The next decade of professional football would begin its new era with the massive use of television, a new commissioner, and the birth of a new enterprise, the American Football League, which would aggressively challenge the NFL.

The incomparable individual brilliance and unique team chemistry that marked this era have transcended this specific time and place to make *Legends of the Hall: 1950s* an unforgettable part of the magic and myth of professional football.

Steve Sabol
President, NFL Films

QUARTERBACKS

Johnny Unitas became a legend after leading Baltimore to an overtime victory over the New York Giants in the 1958 NFL Championship game.

GEORGE BLANDA

George Blanda was enshrined in the Pro Football Hall of Fame in 1981. At six feet, two inches and 215 pounds, Blanda was drafted out of Kentucky. He played both the quarterback and kicker position for the Chicago Bears in 1949, Baltimore Colts in 1950, Chicago Bears from 1950 to 1958, Houston Oilers from 1960 to 1966, and for the Oakland Raiders from 1967 to 1975. In 1970, Blanda was the hero for last-minute comebacks in five straight games. He scored a total of 2,002 points and held or tied for 21 title games—a 16 regular-season mark. In 1961, he passed for seven touchdowns in one game and a total of 36 for the season and was the AFL Player of the Year. In 1970, he was named the AFC Player of the Year.

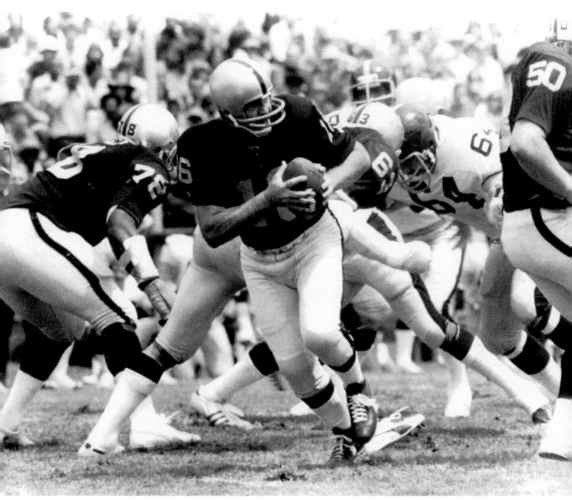

Blanda's career passing totals for his 26 seasons were 4,007 attempts, 26,920 yards received, and 236 touchdowns. Blanda's 26-year, 340-game career was the longest ever in NFL history. He was born September 17, 1927, in Youngwood, Pennsylvania, and played until he was 48. He said, "I never wanted to retire. I was mean and ornery enough to think something might happen."

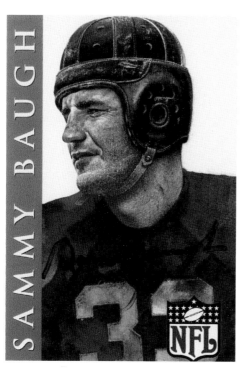

SAMMY BAUGH

Sammy Adrian Baugh was enshrined in the Pro Football Hall of Fame in 1963. At six feet, two inches and 182 pounds, Baugh was drafted out of Texas Christian University as a quarterback. He was a two-time Texas Christian All-America player and was the No. 1 draft choice of the Washington Redskins in 1937 and would hold that position until 1952. He played half his career as a tailback and the other half as a T-quarterback.

As a premier passer, he revolutionized the game. Baugh was All-NFL seven years running. He was also the NFL passing, punting, and interception champ in 1943. Not only was Baugh a six-time NFL passing leader, he was also the top punter in the history of the game. His career record totals are 21,886 yards, 187 touchdowns passing, a 45.1-yard punting average, and 31 interceptions. He was born March 17, 1914, in Temple, Texas.

Leonard Ray Dawson was enshrined in the Pro Football Hall of Fame in 1987. At six feet, 190 pounds, Dawson was drafted out of Perdue as a quarterback in 1957 by the Pittsburgh Steelers. He was their No. 1 draft pick. He played with the Steelers until 1959, and from 1960 to 1961 played for the Cleveland Browns. In 1962, he was traded to the Dallas Texans and led the Texans to an AFL title in 1962. He was also the AFL Player of the Year.

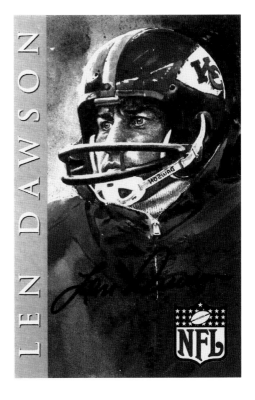

From 1963 through 1975 Dawson was a member of the Kansas City Chiefs, leading them to two (1966 and 1969) AFC titles. He went on to win four AFL passing crowns, was MVP of Super Bowl IV, selected to six AFL All-Star games, and played in the 1972 Pro Bowl game. His career statistics are 28,711 yards, 239 touchdowns, 1,293 yards rushing, and 9 touchdowns rushing. Born June 20, 1935, in Alliance, Ohio, Dawson once said, "You learn by observing for a while, but then you've got to be thrown into the pit."

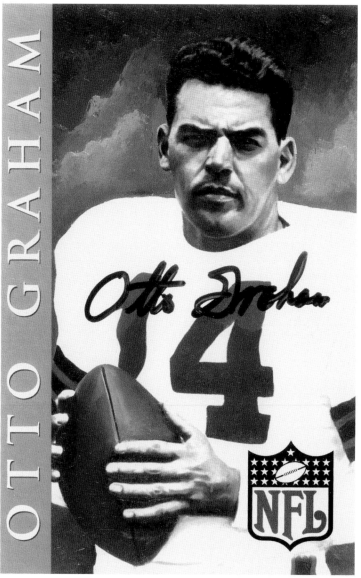

OTTO GRAHAM

Otto Everett Graham Jr. was enshrined in the Pro Football Hall of Fame in 1965. At six feet, one inch and 196 pounds, Graham was drafted out of Northwestern as a tailback in 1946 by the then AAFC Cleveland Browns (1946–1955). He switched to T-quarterback while in the pros. Graham led Browns to 10 division or league crowns in 10 years. He was the top AAFC passer for four years. He was All-League 9 of 10 years. In 1950, the Cleveland Browns joined the NFL. In the 1950 title game, he passed for four touchdowns, beating the Philadelphia Eagles. He was the top NFL passer for two years. In the 1954 NFL title game, Graham had three touchdown's running and three touchdowns passing. His career statistics are 23,584 yards passing, 174 touchdowns, and scored 276 points on 46 touchdowns. He was born December 6, 1921, in Waukegan, Illinois, and died December 17, 2003, at age 82. He once said, "The team concept in football taught me how to work and get along with others while embracing differences to accomplish goals."

Graham rushes for a touchdown.

Graham fights off 49er defender
Bob Toniff.

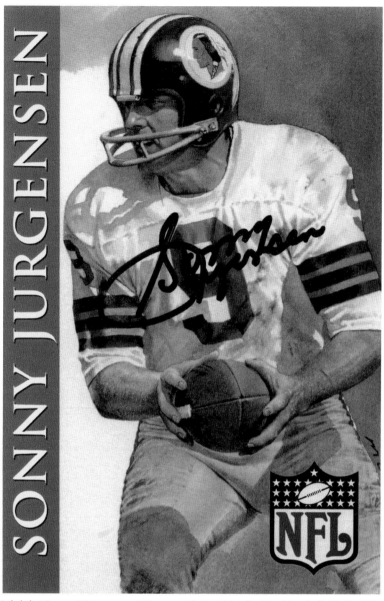

SONNY JURGENSEN

Christian Adolph "Sonny" Jurgensen III was enshrined in the Pro Football Hall of Fame in 1983. At 5 feet, 11 inches and 202 pounds, Jurgensen was drafted out of Duke as a quarterback. He played for the Philadelphia Eagles from 1957 to 1963 and with the Washington Redskins from 1964 to 1974. Sonny was an exceptional passer with outstanding leadership skills and intellect. He was determined, competitive, and poised against the pass rush. He won three NFL individual passing titles and surpassed 3,000 yards in five seasons, 300 yards in 23 games, and 400 yards in five games. His career statistics include 2,433 completions, 32,224 yards, and 255 touchdowns. He excelled in spite of numerous injuries. He was born August 23, 1934, in Wilmington, North Carolina. Sonny once said, "I didn't play in Championship Games or Super Bowls but being selected to the Hall of Fame makes up for all the frustration and disappointment."

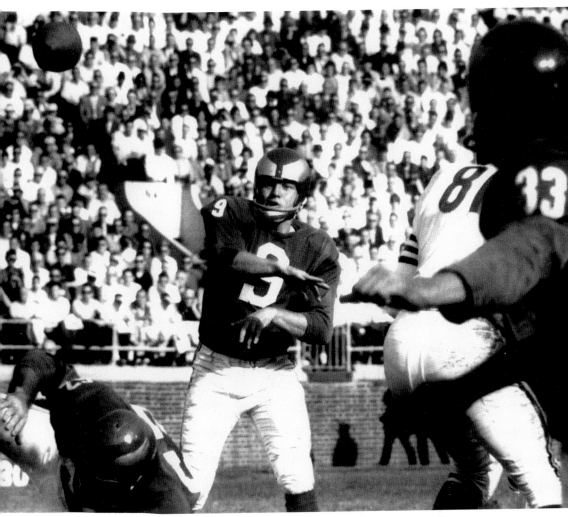

Jurgensen, a premier passer, throws a beautiful pass into the end zone.

Bobby Layne

Robert Lawrence (Bobby) Layne was enshrined in the Pro Football Hall of Fame in 1967. A Texas All-American in 1947, the six foot, one inch, 201 pound Layne was drafted as a quarterback by the Chicago Bears in 1948. In 1949, he played for the New York Bulldogs and from 1950 to 1958. Bobby played for the Detroit Lions where he led the Lions to four division and three NFL titles. Layne was considered to be an exceptional field lead and great under pressure. His last second touchdown pass won the 1953 NFL title game. Layne was also a field-goal kicker. He was All-NFL in 1952 and 1956, second team All-NFL four times, and NFL scoring champ in 1956. He finished his career with the Pittsburgh Steelers from 1958 to 1962. His career statistics include 1,814 completions for 26,768 yards, 196 touchdowns, 2,451 yards rushing, and 372 points scored. He was born December 19, 1926, in Santa Anna, Texas, and died December 1, 1986, at age 59.

Layne may have lived life in the fast lane, but he was always ready for the game. Layne once said, "What I miss more than anything are the guys. I miss training camp, the road trips and the card games. I miss the fellowship, the practice sessions, the locker room, the places where it was a pleasure to be. I miss the bar where we'd go for a beer after practice. I miss the ball games and most of all, I miss my teammates."

Bobby is pictured here in 1954, the same year he made the cover for *Time* magazine.

Sid Luckman

Sidney Luckman was enshrined in the Pro Football Hall of Fame in 1965. A six-foot, 197-pound tailback out of Colombia, he was the No. 1 draft pick by the Chicago Bears in 1939. The Bears turned him into the first great T-quarterback. His performance in a 73-0 title win in 1940 motivated other teams to move to the T-formation. He was All-NFL five times and MVP in 1943. In 1943, he threw seven touchdown passes in one game and five touchdown passes in the 1943 title game. He ended his career with the Bears in 1950. His career statistics include 14,686 yards passing and 137 touchdowns. He was born November 21, 1916, in Brooklyn, New York, and died July 5, 1998, at age 81.

Luckman tries to get a pass off before being hit by an opponent. He once recalled, "I remember when I signed a contract for $5,000, Coach Halas said, 'You and Jesus Christ are the only two people I would ever pay this to.' I said, 'Thank you coach. You put me in great company.'"

Bart Starr

Bryan Bartlett Starr was enshrined in the Pro Football Hall of Fame in 1977. In 1956, the six-foot-one-inch, 197-pound quarterback was drafted by the Green Bay Packers in the 17th round out of Alabama. Starr played for the Packers from 1956 to 1971. He was considered a poised team leader and a precision passer. Starr led the Packers to six division, five NFL, and two Super Bowl titles. He was the NFL's MVP in 1966 and MVP in Super Bowls I and II. Starr was also a three-time NFL passing champion and played in four Pro Bowls. His career statistics include 24,718 yards and 152 touchdowns. He was born January 9, 1934, in Montgomery, Alabama.

A precision passer with the Packers, Bart Starr was also a three-time NFL passing champion. He recalled his great coach: "[Vince] Lombardi was a true genius and a wonderful leader. He taught us the meaning of teamwork and unselfishness, pride and excellence. He once said that long after the trophies are tarnished and the money is spent, the things that you will remember most are the memories of your teammates. How right he was."

Y. A. TITTLE

Yelberton Abraham Tittle was enshrined in the Pro Football Hall of Fame in 1971. Tittle, a great quarterback at six feet, 192 pounds, out of Louisiana State University, was drafted by the Baltimore Colts of the AAFC in 1948. That same year he became the AAFC Rookie of the Year. Tittle joined the San Francisco 49ers in 1951, after the Colts had disbanded and stayed with the team until 1960. Tittle was traded to the New York Giants in 1961 and won division titles in 1961, 1962, and 1963. He threw 33 touchdown passes in 1962 and 36 in 1963. He was the NFL's MVP in 1961 and 1963 and All-NFL in 1957, 1961, 1962, and 1963. He was elected to seven Pro Bowls. His career statistics include 2,427 completions, 33,070 yards, 242 touchdowns, and 13 games over 300 yards passing. He was born October 24, 1926, in Marshall, Texas.

Tittle was a standout with both the San Francisco 49ers and New York Giants. He once said, "The Hall of Fame is truly the biggest thrill of my life because I have sincerely loved football all of my life."

Johnny Unitas

John Constantine Unitas was enshrined in the Pro Football Hall of Fame in 1979. The six-foot-one-inch, 194-pound quarterback out of Louisville was drafted by the Pittsburgh Steelers in 1955 but was immediately cut by the Steelers and became a free agent with the Baltimore Colts in 1956. Unitas stayed with the Colts until 1972. He became a legendary hero. He was an exceptional field leader who thrived under pressure. He led the Colts to NFL crowns in 1958 and 1959 and a Super Bowl V victory. Unitas was All-NFL six seasons, Player of the Year three times, and MVP three times in 10 Pro Bowls. He ended his career in 1973 playing for the San Diego Chargers. His career statistics include 2,830 passes for 40,239 yards, 290 touchdowns, and at least one touchdown pass in 47 straight games. He had 26 games over 300 yards passing. He was born May 7, 1933, in Pittsburgh and died September 11, 2002, at age 69.

QUARTERBACKS

Gridiron general Johnny Unitas hands off to another Colt player. He once recalled, "I will never forget some of the great players I have played with over the years, Lenny Moore, Raymond Berry, Gino Marchetti, Art Donovan, Jim Parker and John Mackey who are directly responsible for me being here at the Hall of Fame."

Norm Van Brocklin

Norman Mack Van Brocklin was enshrined in the Pro Football Hall of Fame in 1971. An All-America quarterback in 1948 out of Oregon, Van Brocklin was the Los Angeles Rams' No. 4 draftee in 1949. Norm remained with the Rams until 1957. In 1951, he threw a 73-yard pass to give the Rams the 1951 title. That same year he passed for 554 yards in one game. He led the NFL in passing three years and in punting two years. From 1958 to 1960, Van Brocklin was the field general for the Philadelphia Eagles and in 1960 led them to the NFL crown. He was also named the NFL's MVP that year. Norm played in nine Pro Bowls. His career statistics include 1,553 completions for 23,611 yards and 173 touchdowns. He was born March 15, 1926, in Eagle Butte, South Dakota, and died May 2, 1983, at age 57.

Van Brocklin was an explosive passer with an explosive temper. He once described his play: "As a quarterback, I called all my own plays . . . not the coach. The quarterback is the only person who can get the actual feel of the play on the field. He is the leader of the team."

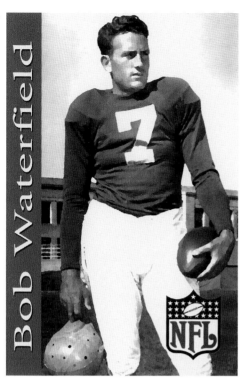

Bob Waterfield

Robert Stanton Waterfield was enshrined in the Pro Football Hall of Fame in 1965. The six-foot-one-inch, 200-pound quarterback out of UCLA was the Cleveland Rams' No. 5 future draft pick in 1944. In 1945, Waterfield was the NFL's MVP rookie. His career statistics include 11,849 yards, 97 touchdowns passing, 573 points on 13 touchdowns, 315 PATs, 60 field goals, and a 42.4-yard punting average.

Waterfield was not only the quarterback but also played defense his first four years with the team. He said, "If I were just coming into professional football today I think I'd still be a quarterback. I'd be a pretty rich one, too." He was born July 26, 1920, in Elmira, New York, and died March 25, 1983, at age 62.

QUARTERBACKS

2

RUNNING BACKS

James Nathaniel (Jim) Brown was enshrined in the Pro Football Hall of Fame in 1971. A 1956 All-America fullback out of Syracuse, Brown was Cleveland's No. 1 draft pick in 1957. Brown was six feet, two inches and weighed in at 232 pounds. He led the NFL in rushing for eight years. He was the NFL's MVP in 1958 and 1965 and Rookie of the Year in 1957. He played in nine straight Pro Bowls. He retired from the Browns in 1965.

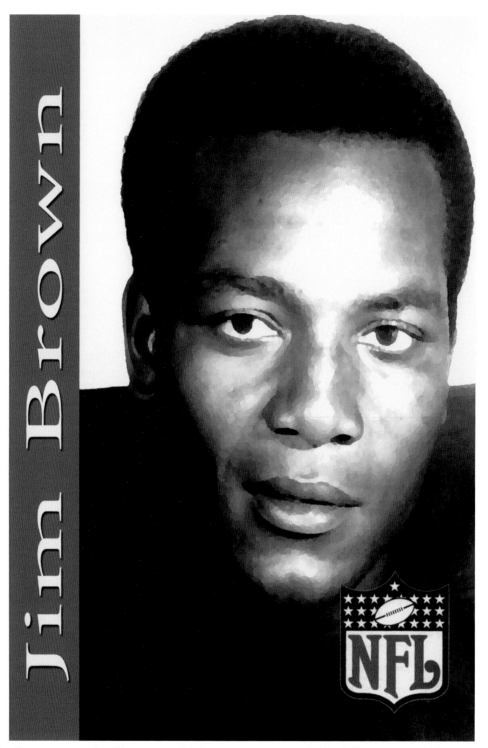

Jim Brown is considered by many to be the greatest running back of all time. In 1957, Brown set a league rushing record in his rookie season.

RUNNING BACKS

Brown's career statistics include 12,312 yards rushing, 262 receptions, 15,459 combined net yards, and 756 points scored. He played with Cleveland his entire career, from 1957 to 1965. He was born February 17, 1936, in St. Simons, Georgia. He said, "I always loved this country and always had a loyalty and respect for it. When the National Anthem is being played that is the time for me to pay respect to this country for the opportunity it has afforded me to play this great game."

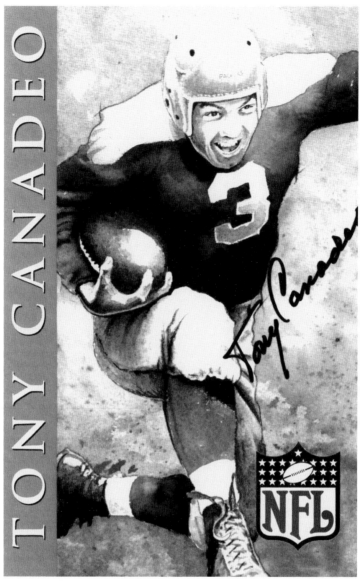

TONY CANADEO

Anthony Robert (Tony) Canadeo was enshrined in the Pro Football Hall of Fame in 1974. A 5-foot-11-inch, 190-pound fullback out of Gonzaga, Canadeo was Little All-America in 1939. He was drafted by the Green Bay Packers in 1941 and played out his career with the team from 1941 to 1944 and 1946 to 1953. Canadeo was a multitalented, two-way performer. He averaged 75 yards in all categories in 116 NFL games. He led the Packers' air game in 1943 and upon return from the service in 1946, was utilized as a heavy-duty runner. Tony became the third back to pass the 1,000-yard mark in one season—1949. He was All-NFL in 1943 and 1949. His career statistics are 4,197 yards rushing, 1,642 yards passing, 186 points, and 69 pass receptions. He was born May 5, 1919, in Chicago and died November 29, 2003, at age 84. He said, "The Hall of Fame was my dream. My dream came true and I share it with my former teammates and fans because it is partly theirs."

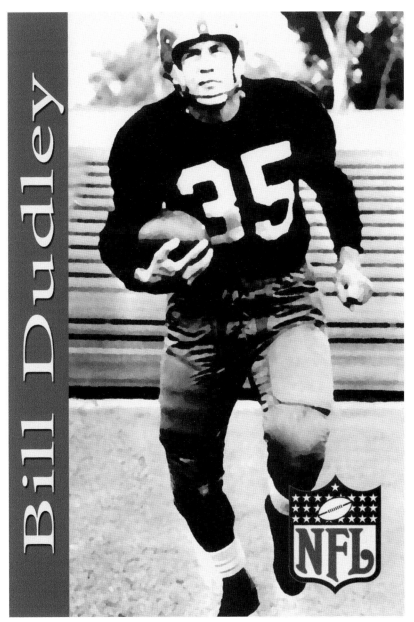

William McGarvey (Bill) Dudley was enshrined in the Pro Football Hall of Fame in 1966. In 1941, the 5-foot-10-inch, 182-pound halfback was Virginia's first All-American. Dudley was the Steelers' No. 1 draft choice in 1942. He was small yet versatile. He won the rare triple crown (NFL rushing, interception, and punt return titles) in 1946. Bill was All-NFL in 1941 and 1946 and was the MVP for 1946. He played for the Pittsburgh Steelers in 1942 and from 1945 to 1946, the Detroit Lions from 1947 to 1949, and the Washington Redskins from 1950 to 1951, 1953. His career statistics include 8,217 combined yards, 478 points, and 23 interceptions. He was born December 24, 1921, in Bluefield, Virginia. He said, "Football meant a college education which opened all the doors in life—opportunity, a career, marriage and a comfortable retirement."

Frank Gifford

Frank Newton Gifford was enshrined in the Pro Football Hall of Fame in 1977. A six-foot-one-inch, 197-pound All-America halfback at the University of Southern California, Gifford was the No. 1 draft pick of the New York Giants in 1952. He played with the Giants from 1952 to 1960 and 1962 to 1964. He was an outstanding player on both offense and defense. Frank was All-NFL for four years and NFL Player of the Year in 1956. He played in seven Pro Bowl games as a defensive back, halfback, and flanker. Gifford retired in 1961 only to return in 1962, but this time as a flanker. His career statistics include 9,862 combined yards total including 3,609 yards rushing, 367 receptions, and 484 points. He was born August 16, 1930, in Santa Monica, California.

Gifford (also known as Mr. Versatile) was a great halfback and receiver.

Gifford was also an outstanding defensive player who once said, "Even though I was the number one draft pick of the New York Giants, I really didn't know what I was stepping into and I wasn't sure that I could play professional football."

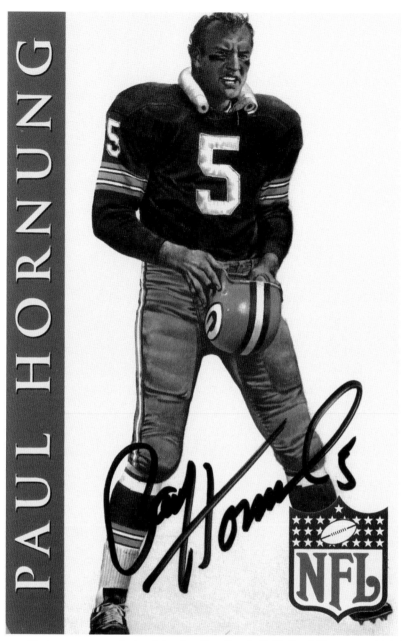

PAUL HORNUNG

Paul Vernon Hornung was enshrined in the Pro Football Hall of Fame in 1986. Hornung was the 1957 Heisman Trophy winner and All-America halfback out of Notre Dame. At six feet, two inches and 215 pounds, he was the bonus draft pick of the Green Bay Packers in 1957. Hornung's career with the Packers spanned from 1957 to 1962 and 1964 to 1966. This multitalented player was NFL Player of the Year in 1960 and 1961. He led the NFL in scoring three years with a record 176 points in 1960. Hornung played in two Pro Bowls and tallied a record 19 points in the 1961 NFL title game. His career statistics are 3,711 yards rushing, 130 receptions, and 760 points. He was born December 23, 1935, in Louisville, Kentucky.

Green Bay's "Golden Boy" was a great runner who loved "life in the fast lane." He once said, "When I was playing for Green Bay, we had to stay with the same team. The camaraderie, the love that our teammates had for one another lasted throughout all these years. That's very, very important to a team. And that is one of the reasons why the Packers were so successful. That's why there were dynasties."

JOHN HENRY JOHNSON

John Henry Johnson was enshrined in the Pro Football Hall of Fame in 1987. The six-foot-two-inch, 210-pound fullback out of Arizona State University was the Steelers' No. 2 draft pick in 1953. In 1954, he joined the San Francisco 49ers after playing a year in Canada. He was part of San Francisco's Million Dollar Backfield along with Hugh McElhenny, Joe Perry, and Y. A. Tittle. He was a powerful runner and outstanding blocker. In 1960, Johnson was traded to Pittsburgh where he surpassed 1,000 yards rushing in 1962 and 1964. Johnson's career spanned over four teams, San Francisco 49ers from 1954 to 1956, the Detroit Lions from 1957 to 1959, the Pittsburgh Steelers from 1960 to 1965, and the Houston Oilers in 1966. His career statistics include 6,803 yards, 48 touchdowns rushing, 186 receptions for 1,478 yards, and seven touchdowns. He was born November 24, 1929, in Waterproof, Louisiana.

A member of the Million Dollar Backfield, Johnson was one tough running back. He once said, "There is more to playing fullback than just running. How many times does a back peel off a long run by himself? I'll tell you—absolutely none!"

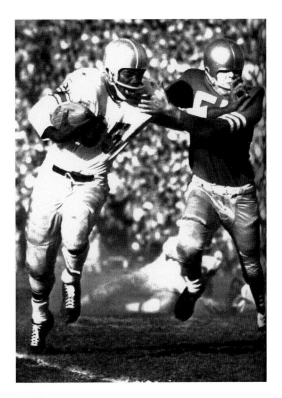

Against league rival the Los Angeles Rams, San Francisco's John Henry Johnson would either run by or run over his rivals.

Ollie Genoa Matson was enshrined in the Pro Football Hall of Fame in 1972. A six-foot-two-inch, 220-pound halfback, Matson was a defensive All-American out of the University of San Francisco. He was a 1952 U.S. Olympic medal winner in track. That same year, he was the No. 1 draft pick of the Chicago Cardinals, whom he played with in 1952 and from 1954 to 1958. Matson was All-NFL from 1954 to 1957. He was traded to the Los Angeles Rams for nine players in 1959. He played in six Pro Bowl games and was the Pro Bowl MVP in 1956. Matson played for the Rams from 1959 to 1962, the Detroit Lions in 1963, and the Philadelphia Eagles from 1964 to 1966. His career statistics include 12,884 combined net yards, 5,173 yards rushing, 222 receptions, 438 points, and 9 touchdowns on punt and kickoff returns. He was born May 1, 1930, in Trinity, Texas.

Known as "All the Way Ollie," Matson is seen here on his way to the end zone.

Matson's speed and quickness were second to none in the NFL. He once said, "Speed and quickness—that's what you need to return kicks. I could either run around you, over you, or through you. I had that peripheral vision to know where guys were going to be and I had the speed to get there."

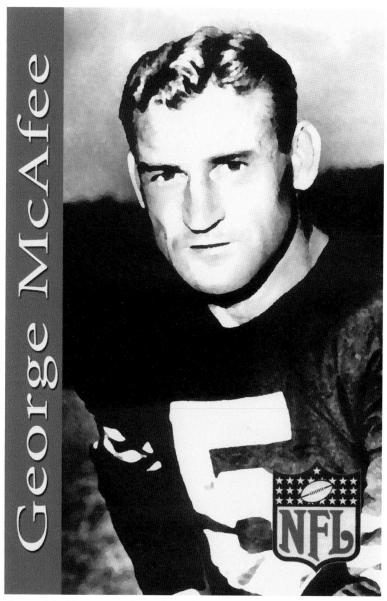

George McAfee

George Anderson McAfee was enshrined in the Pro Football Hall of Fame in 1966. Out of Duke, the six-foot, 178-pound halfback was a phenomenal two-way star. He was drafted by the Chicago Bears in 1940 and was All-NFL in 1941. McAfee served in the U.S. Navy until 1945 before returning to the Bears, where he played until 1950. In 1948, McAfee was the NFL punt return champion. He was also a left-handed passer and kicker. He was the first one to wear low-cut shoes. His career statistics include 234 points scored, 5,313 combined net yards, and intercepted 25 passes in eight seasons. He was born March 13, 1918, in Corbin, Kentucky. He once said, "My biggest game was that 1940 championship against Washington. The Redskins had beaten us 7-3 three weeks before in Washington. To come back and beat them 73-0 for the championship was a great thrill."

RUNNING BACKS

McAfee on a punt return looks like he is literally running over his defenders.

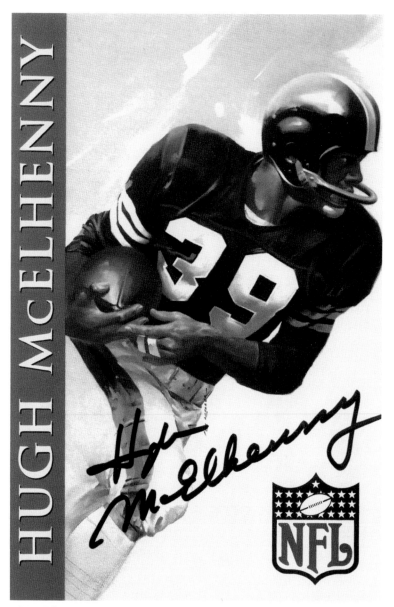

HUGH McELHENNY

Hugh Edward McElhenny Jr. was enshrined in the Pro Football Hall of Fame in 1970. An outstanding halfback out of Washington, at six feet, one inch and 195 pounds, McElhenny was an All-American and the San Francisco 49ers No. 1 draft pick in 1952. He scored a 40-yard touchdown on his first professional play. Nicknamed "the King," McElhenny won All-NFL Rookie of the Year honors and played in six Pro Bowl games. As part of the 49ers' Million Dollar Backfield, he was the MVP of the 1958 Pro Bowl. His career statistics include 5,281 yards rushing, 264 pass receptions, 360 points, and a total 11,375 combined net yards in 13 years. McElhenny played for the San Francisco 49ers from 1952 to 1960, the Minnesota Vikings from 1961 to 1962, the New York Giants in 1963, and the Detroit Lions in 1964. He was born December 31, 1928, in Los Angeles, California.

The King takes a handoff from 49ers' quarterback Y. A. Tittle. He once said, "Football's a great life. The 50s was the cornerstone, I believe, of what pro football is today."

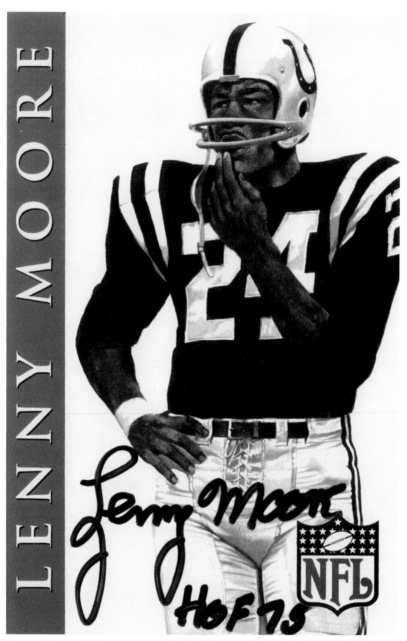

LENNY MOORE

Leonard Edward (Lenny) Moore was enshrined in the Pro Football Hall of Fame in 1975. A Pennsylvania State University flanker, Moore was the 1956 No. 1 draft choice of the Baltimore Colts where he remained until 1967. He was Rookie of the Year in 1956 and was moved to the running back position in 1961. Moore was All-NFL for five years, played in seven Pro Bowls, and was Comeback Player of the Year in 1964. He scored touchdowns in a record 18 straight games—1963–1965. His career statistics include 12,451 combined net yards, 5,174 yards rushing, 363 receptions for 6,039 yards, and scored 113 touchdowns for 678 points. He was born November 25, 1933, in Reading, Pennsylvania.

Tackle Jim Parker leads Lenny Moore on an end around for the score. Moore once said, "I used to come on the field and look around the stands and see all these people during the pre-game warm-up. I'd say to myself, 'I don't believe this . . . I'm a Baltimore Colt!' And I would be pulling at my jersey, looking at that blue."

MARION MOTLEY

Marion Motley was enshrined in the Pro Football Hall of Fame in 1968. This six-foot-one-inch, 232-pound fullback was drafted out of Nevada by the Cleveland Browns (AAFC/NFL) in 1946. He remained with the Browns until 1953. He played with the Pittsburgh Steelers in 1955. Motley was a deadly pass blocker who also played linebacker early in his career. He was the all-time AAFC rushing champ and in 1950 was the top NFL rusher. Marion was All-AAFC for four years and All-NFL in 1950. He played in the 1951 Pro Bowl. His career statistics are caught 85 passes, scored 234 points in nine years, and held a lifetime rushing record of 828 carriers for 4,720 yards. He was born June 5, 1920, in Leesburg, Georgia, and died June 27, 1999, at age 79.

Motley played both the fullback and linebacker positions equally well. He once said, "I always had the feeling I should have carried the ball more but Paul Brown was a winner and he didn't need any advice from me."

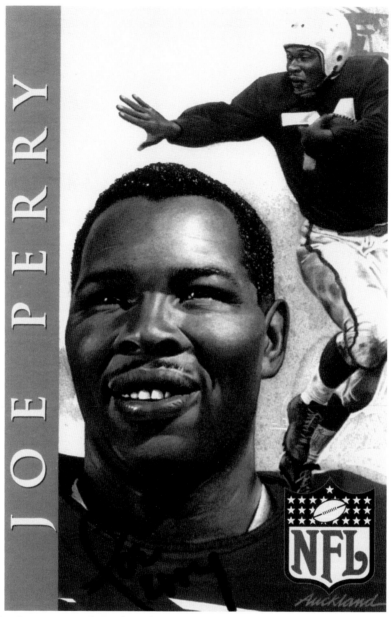

Fletcher Joe Perry was enshrined in the Pro Football Hall of Fame in 1969. Perry attended Compton Junior College but did not play college football. He was playing fullback while in the service (at six feet, 200 pounds) when professional scouts spotted him. He was signed as a free agent by the San Francisco 49ers (AAFC/NFL) in 1948. As part of San Francisco's famed Million Dollar Backfield, Joe was a fabulous runner who was nicknamed "the Jet." He played in three Pro Bowls and was the first to gain over 1,000 yards two years straight, 1953–1954. Perry played for the 49ers from 1948 to 1960 and for the Baltimore Colts from 1961 to 1962. He ended his career with the 49ers in 1963. His career statistics include 12,532 combined net yards, 9,723 yards rushing, 260 receptions, and 513 points. He was born January 22, 1927, in Stevens, Arkansas.

RUNNING BACKS

Catching a screen pass from Y. A. Tittle and going all the way for a touchdown, Joe the Jet was a member of the 49ers' Million Dollar Backfield. Perry once said, "Football was the opening of doors and the teaching of ethics, manners and teamwork. Today's young people could adhere to that."

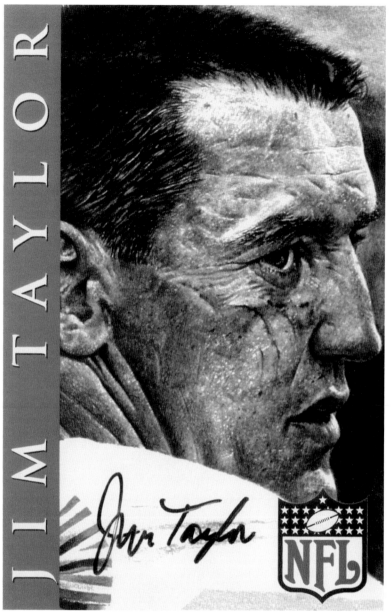

JIM TAYLOR

James Charles (Jim) Taylor was enshrined in the Pro Football Hall of Fame in 1976. Taylor was a 1957 All-American out of Louisiana State University. The six-foot, 214-pound fullback was the No. 2 draft pick of the Green Bay Packers in 1958. He was considered a ferocious runner and blocker and was a disciple of the "run to daylight" doctrine. Taylor was a 1,000-yard rusher for five straight years, from 1960 to 1964. He led the NFL in rushing and scoring and had a record 19 touchdowns in 1962. Taylor was a standout in the 1962 NFL title game. He played with the Packers from 1958 to 1966 and with the New Orleans Saints in 1967. His career statistics include 8,597 yards rushing, 225 receptions, 10,539 combined net yards, and scored 558 points. He was born September 20, 1935, in Baton Rouge, Louisiana.

A muddy Taylor runs to daylight. He described his football philosophy: "Football really is a matter of inches. It was between the defense and me. The best man won and no one was going to hit me harder than I hit them."

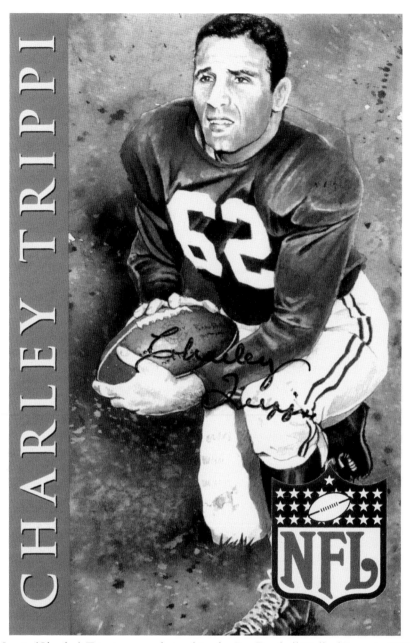

CHARLEY TRIPPI

Charles Louis (Charley) Trippi was enshrined in the Pro Football Hall of Fame in 1968. Trippi was the Chicago Cardinals' No. 1 future draft pick in 1945. He was a Georgia All-American in 1946 and played in four Chicago All-Star games as a collegian. In 1947, he signed with the Cards during the AAFC-NFL war for the unheard of amount of $100,000. Charley became the final link to the Cards' famed Dream Backfield. He scored two touchdowns in the 1947 NFL title win. He was All-NFL in 1948. Trippi was an extremely versatile player. He played the halfback position for five years, the quarterback position for two years, and defense for two years. He ended his career with the Cardinals in 1955. He was born December 14, 1922, in Pittston, Pennsylvania.

Trippi once said, "Football has enriched my life in so many ways giving me ambition, making me set goals—but the Hall was the greatest goal."

STEVE VAN BUREN

Stephen W. Van Buren was enshrined in the Pro Football Hall of Fame in 1965. Louisiana State University's six-foot, 200-pound halfback was the No. 1 draft pick of the Philadelphia Eagles in 1944. He was All-NFL for six straight years, won the NFL rushing title four times, was the 1944 punt return champ, and the 1945 kick off return champ. Van Buren scored the only touchdown in a 7-0 title win in 1948. He rushed twice for over 1,000 yards. Steve played for the Eagles from 1944 to 1951. His career statistics include 5,860 yards rushing and 464 points scored. He was born December 28, 1920, in La Ceiba, Honduras. He said, "Money meant nothing to me when it came to playing football. I was stupid—that's why."

Van Buren was Philadelphia's No. 1 draft pick in 1944.

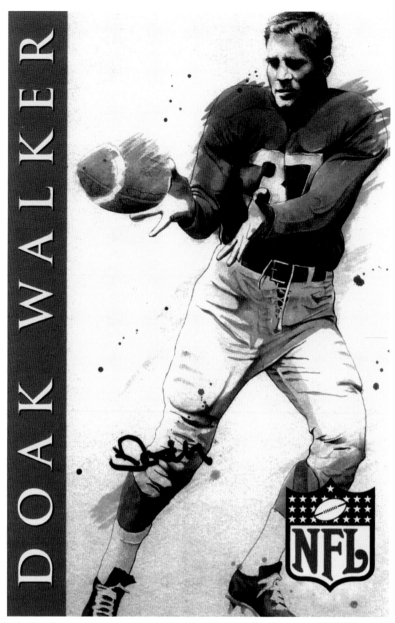

DOAK WALKER

Ewell Doak Walker Jr. was enshrined in the Pro Football Hall of Fame in 1986. This 5-foot-11-inch, 173-pound halfback and three-time All-American out of Southern Methodist University was also the 1948 Heisman Trophy winner. Drafted by the Lions in 1950, Walker played a major role in the success of the Lions in the early part of the 1950s. In the 1952 title game, Walker ran for 67 yards for the winning touchdown. His versatility included rushing, passing, catching, returning punts and kickoffs, punting, placekicking, and playing defense when needed. Walker won two NFL scoring titles, was All-NFL five years, and played in five Pro Bowls. He scored a total of 534 points in his career with Detroit (1950–1955). He was born January 1, 1927, in Dallas, Texas, and died September 27, 1998, at age 71.

Walker played all positions on both offense and defense. He once said, "We played for the fun of the game and a loyalty to our club and teammates. I played football because I loved the game and the camaraderie."

The famed San Francisco 49ers' Million Dollar Backfield with Hugh McElhenny, Joe Perry, Y. A. Tittle, and John Henry Johnson.

RUNNING BACKS

3

TIGHT ENDS AND WIDE RECEIVERS

Raymond Berry
could always be
counted on to
make the big plays.

RAYMOND BERRY

Raymond Emmett Berry was enshrined in the Pro Football Hall of Fame in 1973. Berry was an exceptional end out of Southern Methodist University. At six feet, two inches and 187 pounds, he was the Colts' 20th round future draft choice in 1954. Beginning his professional career in 1955, Raymond was a favorite passing choice of quarterback Johnny Unitas. He was All-NFL from 1958 to 1960, elected to six Pro Bowls, and set an NFL title game mark with 12 catches for 178 yards in the famous 1958 overtime game against the New York Giants. Berry played with the Baltimore Colts from 1955 to 1967. His career statistics include a record 631 passes for 9,275 yards and 68 touchdowns. He was born February 27, 1933, in Corpus Christi, Texas.

Berry was at his best when Johnny Unitas was leading the Colts in the final minutes of a game. He once said, "When I came into the NFL the furthest thing from my mind was making the Hall of Fame. I just wanted to make the Colts' team for a couple of years. I think that the most fortunate thing that has ever happened to me was being able to play pro football in the era that I had played."

TOM FEARS

Thomas Jesse Fears was enshrined in the Pro Football Hall of Fame in 1970. A six-foot-two-inch, 216-pound end out of UCLA, Fears was drafted by the Los Angeles Rams in 1948 and played with them until 1956. He led the NFL as a receiver for the first three seasons, 1948–1950. In 1950, he made 84 catches and had three touchdown receptions in the division title game. He also caught 18 passes in one game. In 1951, he caught a 73-yard pass to win the NFL title game. Fears was All-NFL in 1949 and 1950. His career statistics include 400 catches for 5,397 yards and 38 touchdowns. He was born December 3, 1922, in Guadalajara, Mexico, and died January 4, 2000, at age 77.

In 1950, Fears caught 18 passes
in one game.

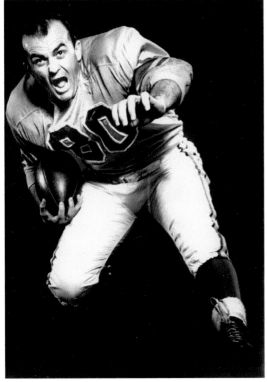

Fears led the NFL in receiving from 1948
to 1950. He once said, "You blocked and
you tackled and you hit with your face
first. That's the way you were taught and
that's the way you did it if you were good.
Your face took one tremendous beating
and if you could hold all your teeth and
not have a broken nose, then you had
to be a 'panty waste'—you weren't doing
your job."

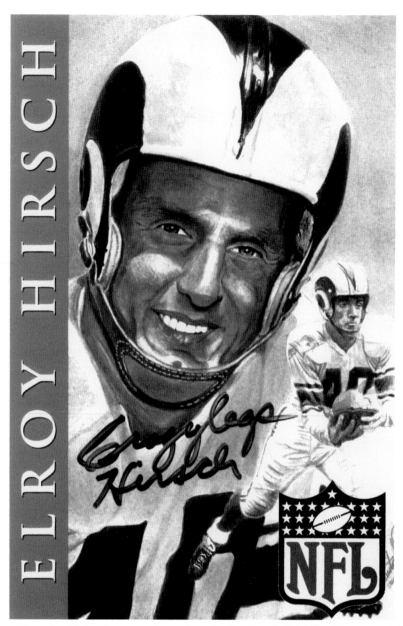

ELROY HIRSCH

Elroy Leon "Crazylegs" Hirsch was enshrined in the Pro Football Hall of Fame in 1968. He led the 1946 College All-Stars upset of the Rams. The six-foot-two-inch, 190-pound end out of Michigan was drafted by the Chicago Rockets (AAFC) in 1946 and stayed with the team until 1948. In 1949, Hirsch began his career with the Los Angeles Rams, which lasted until 1957. He became a key part of the Rams' "three-end" offense. In 1951, Hirsch led the NFL in receiving and scoring. Ten of his 17 touchdown catches were long-distance bombs. Hirsch was elusive and quick. In 1969, he was named the NFL's All-Time Flanker. His career statistics include 387 catches for 7,029 yards, 60 touchdowns, and 399 points scored. He was born June 17, 1923, in Wausau, Wisconsin, and died January 28, 2004, at age 80.

Hirsch is seen here in a public relations photograph for the Chicago Rockets of the AAFC. He once said, "We didn't make anything like the players do today but I have a feeling we had more fun than they do."

As a Los Angeles Ram, Hirsch was the most famous halfback/flanker of the 1950s.

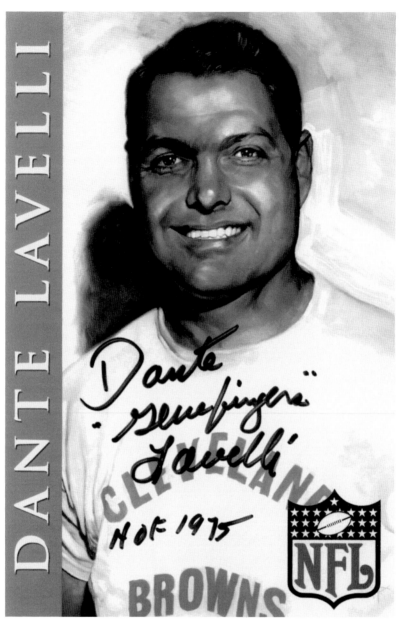

DANTE LAVELLI

Dante Bert Joseph Lavelli was enshrined in the Pro Football Hall of Fame in 1975. This Ohio State University end was drafted by the Cleveland Browns (AAFC/NFL) in 1946. He had played only three college games before serving in the U.S. Army Infantry. At six feet, 191 pounds, Lavelli was the top AAFC receiver as a rookie and scored the winning touchdown in the 1946 title game. He was All-AAFC in 1946 and 1947 and All-NFL in 1951 and 1953. He played in three Pro Bowls. Lavelli caught 11 passes in the 1950 NFL Championship game. He also held a record 24 catches in six NFL title games. His career statistics include 386 receptions for 6,488 yards and 62 touchdowns. Lavelli was nicknamed "Gluefingers." He completed his career with the Browns in 1956. He was born February 23, 1923, in Hudson, Ohio.

Lavelli was nicknamed "Gluefingers" for his great catching ability. He once said, "I'd fare pretty well today against zone defenses. I could catch 20 passes in the flat alone and if Otto was still throwing to me, we'd find a way."

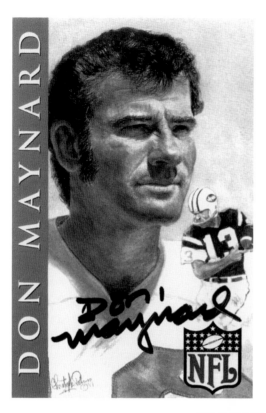

DON MAYNARD

Donald Rogers Maynard was enshrined in the Pro Football Hall of Fame in 1987. Maynard was a six-foot, 180-pound wide receiver out of Texas Western who was drafted by the New York Giants in 1958. In 1960, he signed with the New York Titans/Jets (AFL)—the first signee of the team—where he played until 1972. In five different seasons, Maynard had over 50 catches and 1,000 yards receiving.

A favorite receiver of Joe Namath, Maynard had moves that made him a hard player to tackle. His career statistics include 633 receptions for 11,834 yards, 88 touchdowns, and 532 points. He was born January 25, 1935, in Crosbyton, Texas. He once recalled, "I told Giants' coach, Allie Sherman that I could cover more ground with one step than anybody could in three. The next day I was cut."

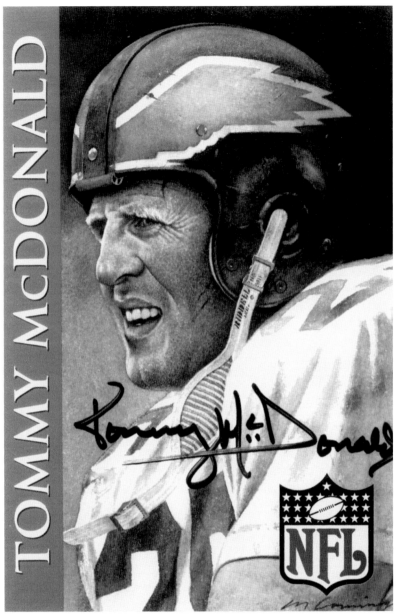

Thomas Franklin McDonald was enshrined in the Pro Football Hall of Fame in 1998. McDonald was the Philadelphia Eagles' third-round draft pick in 1957. Out of Oklahoma, the five-foot-nine-inch, 176-pound wide receiver was selected to six Pro Bowls, scored 56 touchdowns in 63 games (1958–1962), led the NFL in reception yardage and touchdowns in 1961, and ranked sixth all-time in receptions, fourth in yards receiving, and second in touchdown catches at the time of his retirement in 1968. McDonald played with the Eagles from 1957 to 1963, the Dallas Cowboys in 1964, the Los Angeles Rams from 1965 to 1966, the Atlanta Falcons in 1967, and the Cleveland Browns in 1968. His career statistics include 495 receptions, 8,410 yards, and 84 touchdowns. He was born July 26, 1934, in Roy, New Mexico.

Tommy McDonald was on the cover of Sports Illustrated in October 1962. The caption read "Football's Best Hands." He once said, "Paul Hornung once told me that while the Packers were watching game films of the Philadelphia Eagles, Vince Lombardi said to his players, 'If I had 11 Tommy McDonalds, I would win the championship every year!' Coming from such a great coach as Lombardi, that was the greatest compliment that I have ever received."

Robert Cornelius Mitchell was enshrined in the Pro Football Hall of Fame in 1983. Blessed with exceptional speed, balance, and faking ability, this six-foot, 192-pound wide receiver out of Illinois was drafted by the Cleveland Browns in 1958. Mitchell played for the Browns until 1961 and in 1962 signed with the Washington Redskins where he remained until 1968. While with Cleveland, Mitchell played halfback. With the Redskins, he played flanker. He was the top NFL receiver in 1961.

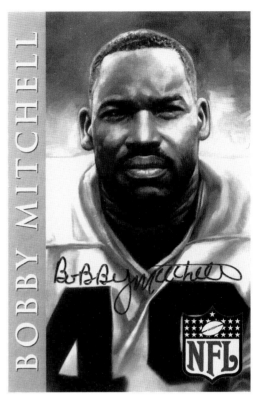

BOBBY MITCHELL

Cleveland's Bobby Mitchell breaks away and runs 40 yards for a touchdown. His career statistics include 91 touchdowns, 521 passes caught, and 8 kick return touchdowns. He was born June 6, 1935, in Hot Springs, Arkansas. Mitchell once recalled, "The reason I made the Browns is because of Jim Brown. I was able to mesh in slowly and was totally relaxed. I don't know what I would have done if he wasn't there."

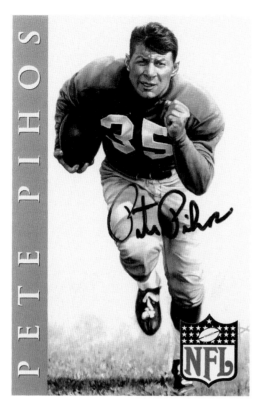

PETE PIHOS

Peter Louis Pihos was enshrined in the Pro Football Hall of Fame in 1970. A six-foot-one-inch, 210-pound end, Pete Pihos was a 1943 All-American out of Indiana. He was a fifth-round draft pick of the Philadelphia Eagles in 1945 even though he could not play until 1947. He caught the winning touchdown pass in the 1949 NFL championship game. Pihos was All-NFL six times in nine seasons—once as a defensive end in 1952—played in six Pro Bowls, and was a three-time NFL receiving champ in 1953, 1954, and 1955.

Pihos was one of the 60-minute stars on the Eagles title teams of 1948–1949. He completed his career with the Eagles in 1955. His career statistics include 373 catches for 5,619 yards and 378 points. He was born October 22, 1923, in Orlando, Florida. He once said, "Football taught me many lessons that gave me the chance to be successful in life."

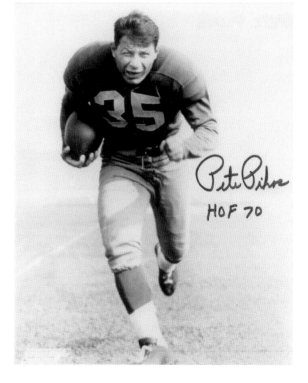

TIGHT ENDS AND WIDE RECEIVERS

4

OFFENSIVE AND
DEFENSIVE LINEMEN

The 49ers' Bob St. Clair excelled in both running and pass blocking.

ROOSEVELT BROWN

Roosevelt Brown Jr. was enshrined in the Pro Football Hall of Fame in 1975. Brown was a black All-American at Morgan State University in 1951 and 1952. He was the Giants' 27th pick in the 1953 draft. The six-foot-three-inch, 255-pound offensive tackle was only 20 years old when he joined the team but quickly won a starting role and held it for 13 seasons. He was fast and mobile, which allowed him to become an excellent downfield blocker and pass protector. Brown was All-NFL eight straight years from 1956 to 1963, and played in nine Pro Bowl games, and was named the NFL's Lineman of the Year in 1956. He ended his career with the Giants in 1965. He was born October 20, 1932, in Charlottesville, Virginia, and died June 9, 2004, at age 71.

Lineman of the Year in 1956, Roosevelt Brown was an excellent downfield blocker and pass protector. He once described his start in football saying, "The football coach thought I was too big to be in the band."

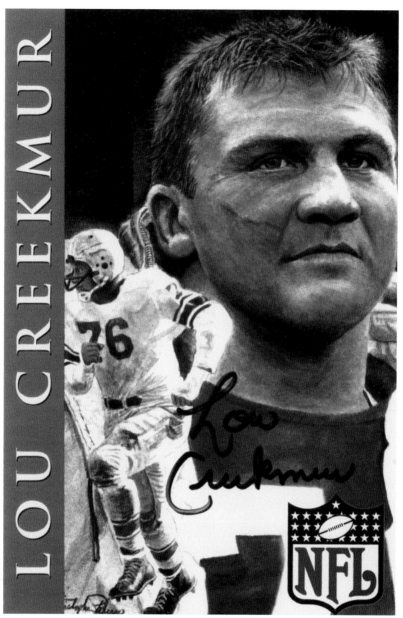

LOU CREEKMUR

Louis Creekmur was enshrined in the Pro Football Hall of Fame in 1996. Creekmur was drafted out of William and Mary and was the No. 2 pick of the Detroit Lions in 1950. At six feet, four inches and 246 pounds, he was flamboyant, versatile, and a strong blocker. He played in 165 straight games from 1950 to 1958. Creekmur was an All-NFL guard in 1951 and 1952; All-NFL tackle in 1953, 1954, 1956, and 1957; selected to eight Pro Bowls, twice as a guard and six times as a tackle; and played on three Lions NFL title teams. He ended his career with Detroit in 1959. He was born January 22, 1927, in Hopelawn, New Jersey. He recalls, "A guy came in and creamed Bobby Layne. Bobby got up and chewed me out in front of 50,000 people. After that, I learned how to keep guys off Bobby."

Detroit's Lou Creekmur was an All-NFL guard whose job was to protect the great Bobby Layne.

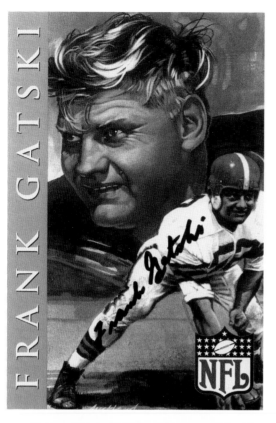

FRANK GATSKI

Frank Gatski was enshrined in the Pro Football Hall of Fame in 1985. A six-foot-three-inch, 233-pound center out of Auburn University, he was a strong, exceptional pass blocker who never missed a game or practice in high school, college, or in the pros. He played in 11 championship games in 12 years. He was All-NFL for four years and played in the 1956 Pro Bowl. His career with Cleveland was from 1946 to 1956 and he played his final year, 1957 with Detroit.

Gatski demonstrates his skill as a lineman with the Browns of the AAFC. He recalled, "I never planned on playing football. It just happened. I loved to play the game. If I could do only one more thing in my life, I would lace up my cleats and play another football game." He was born March 18, 1919, in Farmington, West Virginia, and died November 22, 2005, at age 86.

OFFENSIVE AND DEFENSIVE LINEMEN

Alvis Forrest Gregg was enshrined in the Pro Football Hall of Fame in 1977. Gregg, a six-foot-four-inch, 249-pound tackle out of Southern Methodist University was the No. 2 draft pick of the Green Bay Packers in 1956. Vince Lombardi called him, "the best player I ever coached." He played in 188 straight games from 1956 to 1971, was All-NFL eight straight years from 1960 to 1967, played in nine Pro Bowls, and on seven NFL championships including winning three Super Bowls.

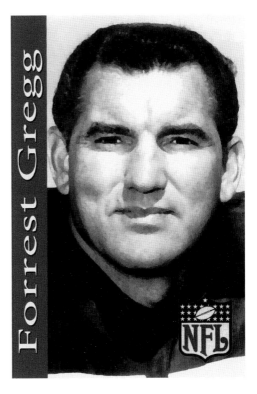

Forrest Gregg

Covered in mud, Gregg encourages the Packer offense from the sidelines. His high caliber of play led him to nine Pro Bowls, seven NFL championships, and three Super Bowls. He was born October 18, 1933, in Birthright, Texas, and once recalled, "I spent 15 years as a player and I don't know how many years I will spend as a coach but I can tell you here and now that this [NFL football] is the greatest business in the world."

LOU GROZA

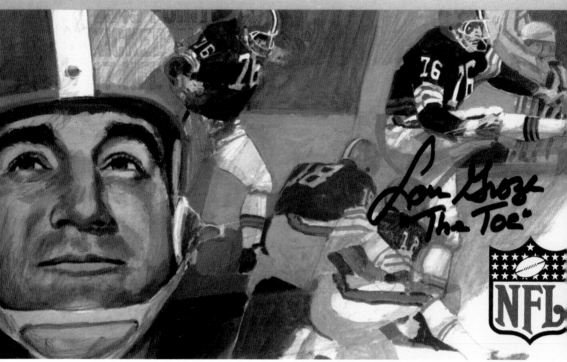

Louis Roy Groza was enshrined in the Pro Football Hall of Fame in 1974. The Cleveland Browns (AAFC/NFL) drafted Groza in 1946. The six-foot-three-inch, 240-pound lineman out of Ohio State University began his career as an offensive tackle but a back injury in 1960 forced him to become a kicking specialist only (1961–1967). He was All-NFL tackle six years and NFL Player of the Year in 1954. He played in nine Pro Bowls and scored a last-second field goal to win the 1950 NFL title game. Groza also played in a total of four AAFC title games and nine NFL title games. He scored 1,608 points in 21 years. His career with the Browns spanned from 1946 to 1959, and 1961 to 1967. He was the last of the "original Browns" to retire. He was born January 25, 1924, in Martins Ferry, Ohio, and died November 29, 2000, at age 76. He said, "Football gave me direction in establishing life's goals."

Gene Hickerson was enshrined in the Pro Football Hall of Fame in 2007. Selected as a future draft choice by the Browns in 1957, Hickerson played guard at Mississippi. A six-foot-three-inch, 248-pound tackle in college, he shifted to guard as a rookie (1958). He was a lead blocker for three future hall of fame running backs Jim Brown, Bobby Mitchell, and Leroy Kelly. Hickerson was All-NFL five consecutive seasons, 1966 to 1970, and was the league's leading rusher seven times. He was born February 15, 1935, in Trenton, Tennessee.

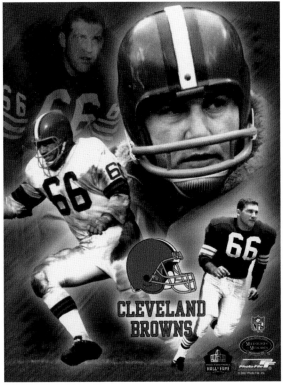

Hickerson played in six straight Pro Bowls and was a lead blocker for Jim Brown, Bobby Mitchell, and Leroy Kelly—all in the hall of fame. He recalls, "I had the good fortune to have been able to block for some of the greatest running backs the NFL has ever had: Jim Brown, Bobby Mitchell and Leroy Kelly."

STAN JONES

Stanley Paul Jones was enshrined in the Pro Football Hall of Fame in 1991. An All-America tackle out of Maryland in 1953 and the Chicago Bears' fifth-round future pick in 1953, Stan Jones began his professional football career as a tackle in 1954 and moved to guard in 1955. In 1962, he shifted to defensive tackle. At six feet, one inch and 252 pounds, he was considered big, quick, disciplined, durable, and intelligent. He was All-NFL in 1955, 1956, 1959, and 1960. He played in seven straight Pro Bowls from 1956 to 1962. Jones was the first player to incorporate weight lifting into his exercise regiment. Stan played with the Bears from 1954 to 1965 and ended his career with the Washington Redskins in 1966. Jones was born November 24, 1931, in Altoona, Pennsylvania.

Jones was one of the NFL's toughest linemen, and recalled playing for a champion: "To be a part of a team that won it all was a real thrill."

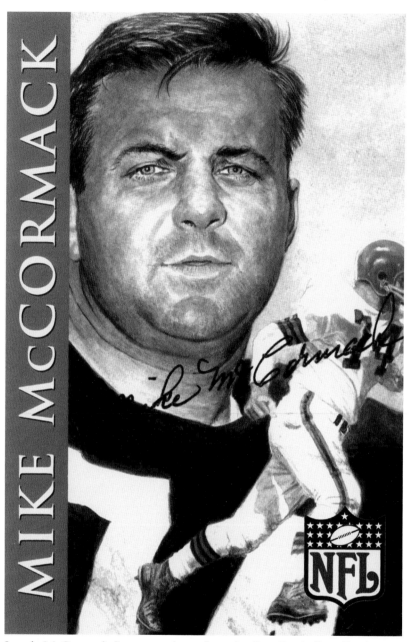

MIKE McCORMACK

Michael Joseph McCormack Jr. was enshrined in the Pro Football Hall of Fame in 1984. McCormack was drafted out of Kansas by the New York Yanks as a tackle in 1951. He served his time in the U.S. Army from 1952 to 1953. While still in the service, McCormack was traded to the Browns in a 15-player deal. In 1954, he played defensive middle guard for the Browns. In the 1954 NFL title game, McCormack stole the ball to set up a key Browns' touchdown. He also excelled at the offensive right tackle position for eight years (1955–1962). His versatility allowed him to become an outstanding rushing blocker and pass protector. McCormack finished out his career with the Browns in 1962. He was born June 21, 1930, in Chicago.

McCormack played in six Pro Bowls, including his rookie season. He recalls football when he played: "You hear a lot of old-timers say they wish they could play in today's era. I don't wish that. I wouldn't trade our era for anyone's."

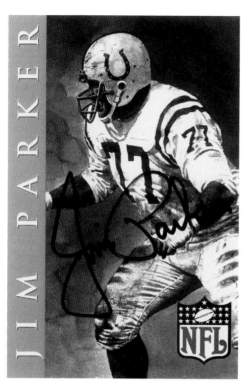

JIM PARKER

James Thomas Parker was enshrined in the Pro Football Hall of Fame in 1973. Jim Parker was a two-time All-America and Outland Trophy winner at Ohio State University. This six-foot-three-inch, 273-pound tackle/guard was the No. 1 draft choice of the Baltimore Colts in 1957. He was All-NFL eight straight years from 1958 to 1965 and played in eight Pro Bowl games. He retired from the Colts in 1967 and was the first full-time offensive lineman named to the Pro Football Hall of Fame.

Parker was a one of the elite blockers of his time and specialized in protecting his team leader, Johnny Unitas. He said, "If I break my arm, I can still play. If Unitas breaks his arm, we're dead. We're just the butter. He is the bread." He was born April 3, 1934, in Macon, Georgia, and died July 18, 2005, at age 71.

James Stephen Ringo was enshrined in the Pro Football Hall of Fame in 1981. Syracuse center, Jim Ringo was the seventh draft choice of the Green Bay Packers in 1953. He was All-NFL seven times, played in 10 Pro Bowls and three NFL championship games. At six feet, two inches and 232 pounds, he was considered small for an offensive lineman but despite numerous injuries, Ringo started in 182 straight games. He played for the Packers from 1953 to 1963 and with the Philadelphia Eagles from 1964 to 1967. He was born November 21, 1931, in Orange, New Jersey.

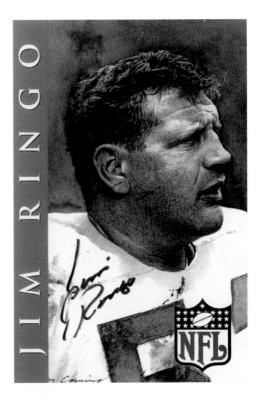

Ringo was one of Green Bay's great offensive lineman but because he brought his agent (which at that time it was unheard of to have an agent) to camp to discuss his contract, Vince Lombardi immediately traded him to the Philadelphia Eagles. He recalls trying to be the best: "I tried to impose self-hypnosis on myself to envision what I had to do on the field and to concentrate to such a degree that I would block out everything else."

BOB ST. CLAIR

Robert Bruce St. Clair was enshrined in the Pro Football Hall of Fame in 1990. This six-foot-nine-inch, 265-pound tackle out of the University of San Francisco, and in his senior year out of Tulsa, was the third-round draft pick of the San Francisco 49ers in 1953. Not only did he have size, but St. Clair had incredible speed, intelligence, and a passion for hitting. He excelled as a running and passing blocker. St. Clair was phenomenal on goal line defense and special teams. He was All-NFL four years and started in five Pro Bowls. In 1956, he blocked 10 field goals. He was the 49ers team captain and nicknamed "Geek" by teammates because of his love for raw meat and his flamboyant lifestyle. St. Clair retired from the 49ers in 1964. He was born February 18, 1931, in San Francisco, California.

St. Clair is pictured here smashing Pittsburgh's Stan Sheriff. He once compared football eras, saying, "I get questions all the time from people wondering how my era would have fared in today's era. Well let's look at it this way. I played both offense and defense predominantly the whole game. We didn't have facemasks the first three years, our helmets were leather and we had numerous injuries where we had to play through. Now, I don't think the question should be whether or not we could play in today's league. I think the question should be whether or not these 'candy asses' of today could play with us!"

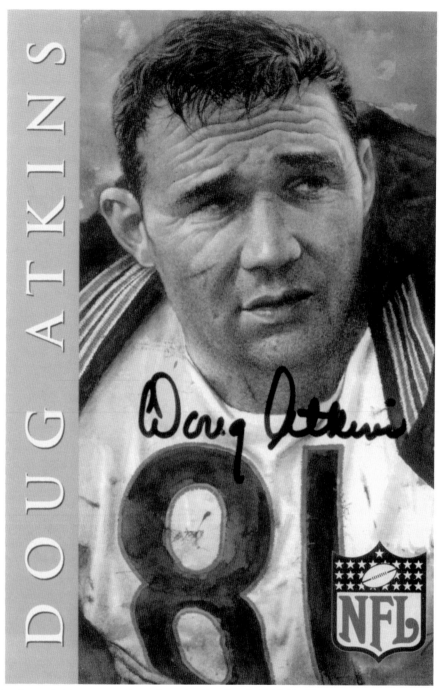

DOUG ATKINS

Douglas Leon Atkins was enshrined in the Pro Football Hall of Fame in 1982. Atkins was an All-America tackle out of Tennessee and the Browns' No. 1 draft pick in 1953. He led the Bears' defensive units for 12 years. Atkins was All-NFL four years and played in eight Pro Bowls. He played with the Cleveland Browns from 1953 to 1954, the Chicago Bears from 1955 to 1966, and the New Orleans Saints from 1967 to 1969.

At six feet, eight inches and 237 pounds, Atkins was one of the most feared defensive players in the league. He once said, "Football gave me the chance to earn a living. Through football I have good friends all over the United States." He was born May 8, 1930, in Humboldt, Tennessee.

WILLIE DAVIS

William Delford Davis was enshrined in the Pro Football Hall of Fame in 1981. Davis was Cleveland's 15th-round draft pick out of Grambling State University in 1956. The six-foot-three-inch, 243-pound defensive end played U.S. Army football prior to his professional career debut with the Browns in 1958. In 1960, he was traded to Green Bay. He was All-NFL five seasons, played in five Pro Bowls, six NFL title games, and two Super Bowls. Davis never missed a game in his 12-year, 162-game career.

Davis was a defensive standout with the Green Bay Packers. He described his love of the game, saying, "I enjoyed football enough that I would have played for nothing—on weekends, in sandlots and open fields. I truly did enjoy it." He played with the Browns until 1959 and from 1960 to 1969 played out his career with the Packers. He was born July 24, 1934, in Lisbon, Louisiana.

OFFENSIVE AND DEFENSIVE LINEMEN

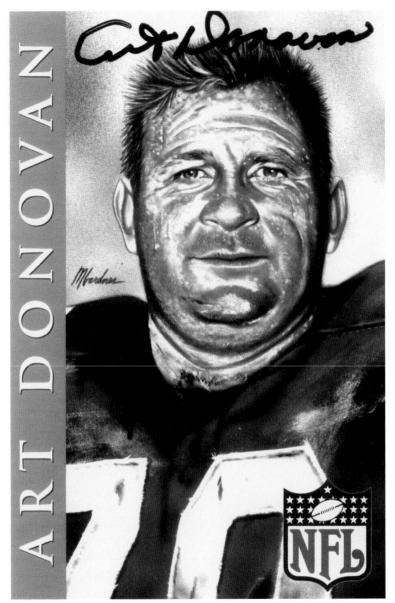

Arthur James Donovan Jr. was enshrined in the Pro Football Hall of Fame in 1968. Artie Donovan was the first Colt to enter the Pro Football Hall of Fame. After serving as a Marine in World War II, the six-foot-two-inch, 263-pound defensive tackle out of Boston College began his career in the NFL as a 26-year-old rookie in 1950. His personality and perseverance made him a vital part of the Baltimore powerhouse of the 1950s. He was All-NFL from 1954 to 1958 and played in five Pro Bowls. He was also the son of famous boxing referee Arthur Donovan Sr. He played for the Baltimore Colts in 1950, the New York Yanks in 1951, the Dallas Texans in 1952, and ended his career with the Baltimore Colts 1953–1961. In reality, all of these teams were the same team, they just changed owners and names over the years. He was born June 5, 1925, in the Bronx, New York.

Art Donovan pursues Giants' quarterback Charlie Connolly. He recalls his good fortune in the game, saying, "Who would have ever thought that of all the kids who played football down through the years and all the grammar schools, high schools and colleges that you would be picked to be lucky enough to play professional football? We look back on that and say that we are lucky that we are here. When we played, men were really men."

Donovan was an outstanding defensive tackle during the Baltimore Colts reign in the late 1950s. Here he is seen with 49er offensive tackle and future hall of fame member Bob St. Clair.

Leonard Guy Ford Jr. was enshrined in the Pro Football Hall of Fame in 1976. The six-foot-four-inch, 245-pound defensive end out of Michigan caught 67 passes as a two-way end with the Los Angeles Dons (AAFC) from 1948 to 1949. Upon the demise of the AAFC, the Cleveland Browns converted him to a full-time defensive end. Ford was an exceptional pass rusher, and after overcoming serious injuries in 1950, earned All-NFL honors five times from 1951 to 1955 and played in four Pro Bowls. He recovered 20 opponents' fumbles throughout his NFL career. He played with the Cleveland Browns from 1950 to 1957 and retired from the Green Bay Packers in 1958. He was born February 18, 1926, in Washington, D.C., and died March 14, 1972, at age 46. He recalls, "I used to love running over guys. You just have to expect some of that rough stuff every game or you won't last long."

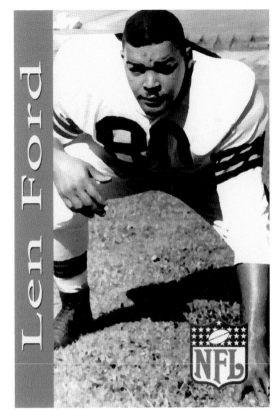

Henry Wendell Jordan was enshrined in the Pro Football Hall of Fame in 1995. This six-foot-two-inch, 248-pound defensive tackle out of Virginia was Cleveland's fifth-round draft pick in 1957. He was traded to the Green Bay Packers for a fourth-round pick in 1959. He became an 11-year starter at right defensive tackle. Jordan was All-NFL six times, played in four Pro Bowls, and seven NFL title games as well as in Super Bowls I and II. He missed only two games throughout his first 12 seasons. His career with the Cleveland Browns spanned from 1957 to 1958 and with the Packers from 1959 to 1969. He was born January 26, 1935, in Emporia, Virginia, and died February 21, 1977, at age 42. He once said, "I guess you realize I'm the only player on the Packers who's not afraid of Vince Lombardi. Seriously now. Coach Lombardi is very fair. He treats us all the same way . . . like dogs."

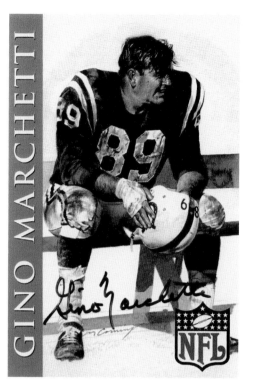

GINO MARCHETTI

Gino John Marchetti was enshrined in the Pro Football Hall of Fame in 1972. Gino, a six-foot-four-inch, 244-pound defensive end out of the University of San Francisco was the New York Yanks' No. 2 draft pick in 1952. He played in 11 straight Pro Bowls but missed one game because of a broken leg that was sustained in the 1958 NFL overtime title game against the Giants. He was born January 2, 1927, in Smithers, West Virginia.

Marchetti was well known throughout the league as a vicious pass rusher and was named Top Defensive End of the NFL's First Fifty Years. He describes playing hurt, "I was taped up on one side and I could use only one arm. I hurt like hell but they had no replacement for me, so I went out and played."

LEO NOMELLINI

Leo Joseph Nomellini was enshrined in the Pro Football Hall of Fame in 1969. A two-time defensive tackle All-American out of Minnesota, the six-foot-three-inch, 259-pound Nomellini was the 49ers' first ever NFL draft choice in 1950. He played every 49ers game for 14 seasons. He was named the NFL's All-Time Defensive Tackle and played in 10 Pro Bowl games. Nomellini ended his career with the 49ers in 1963. He was born June 19, 1924, in Lucca, Italy, and died October 17, 2000, at age 76.

Leo "the Lion" Nomellini is shown here tackling Colts' quarterback Johnny Unitas. He once recalled, "Canton is thousands of miles from Lucca, Italy—the place I was born. But my induction into the Hall shows the opportunities and sportsmanship that exist in America."

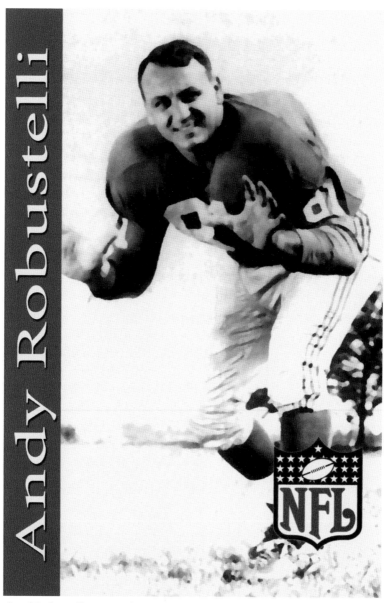

Andy Robustelli

Andrew Richard Robustelli was enshrined in the Pro Football Hall of Fame in 1971. Robustelli was a six-foot-one-inch, 230-pound defensive end out of Arnold College. He was the Los Angeles Rams' 19th-round draft pick in 1951. A superb pass rusher, Robustelli was exceptionally quick, strong, and smart. Missing only one game in his 14-year career, he recovered 22 opponents' fumbles. He played in eight NFL title games, seven Pro Bowls, was All-NFL seven years—two with the Rams and five with the Giants—and named the NFL's top player by the Maxwell Club in 1962. Robustelli played with the Rams from 1951 to 1955 and with the New York Giants from 1956 to 1964. He was born December 6, 1925, in Stamford, Connecticut. He once recalled, "I loved to go to the store for my mother because when she needed Italian bread, it looked like a football and I could toss it in the air and take it home for a touchdown."

Ernest Alfred Stautner was enshrined in the Pro Football Hall of Fame in 1969. This Bavarian-born defensive tackle out of Boston College was the No. 2 draft pick of the Pittsburgh Steelers in 1950. At six feet, one inch and 230 pounds, he anchored the strong Pittsburgh defense for 14 years. He was All-NFL in 1955, 1956, 1958, and 1959 and played in nine Pro Bowls. In 1957, Stautner won the Best Lineman Award. He was born April 20, 1925, in Prinzing-by-Cham, Bavaria, and died February 16, 2006, at age 80.

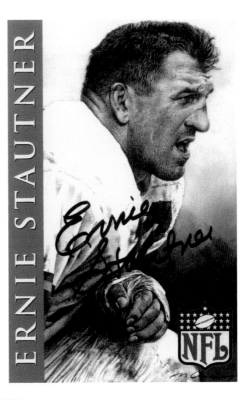

ERNIE STAUTNER

Extremely strong and tough, Stautner was feared in the league by many offensive players. He recalls, "It gave me great satisfaction to succeed in professional football after being told by many coaches that I was too small."

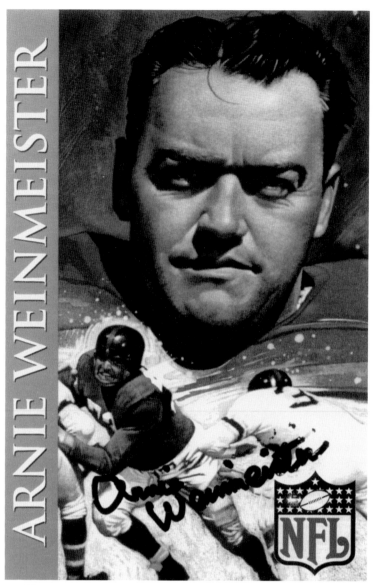

Arnold George Weinmeister was enshrined in the Pro Football Hall of Fame in 1984. Arnie Weinmeister was an extremely fast, six-foot-four-inch, 235-pound defensive tackle out of Washington. He began his professional football career with the New York Yankees (AAFC) in 1948 and ended his career with the New York Giants in 1953. Weinmeister played two ways in the AAFC, but played exclusively on defense with the NFL. He became the dominant defensive tackle of his time. Weinmeister was All-AAFC in 1949, All-NFL from 1950 to 1953, and named to four Pro Bowls. He played for the New York Yankees (AAFC) in 1948, the Brooklyn–New York Yankees in 1949 (AAFC), and the New York Giants from 1950 to 1953. He was born March 23, 1923, in Rhein, Saskatchewan, and died June 29, 2000, at age 77. He recalled his era: "It was a different game when I played. When a player made a good play, he didn't jump up and down. Those kinds of plays were expected."

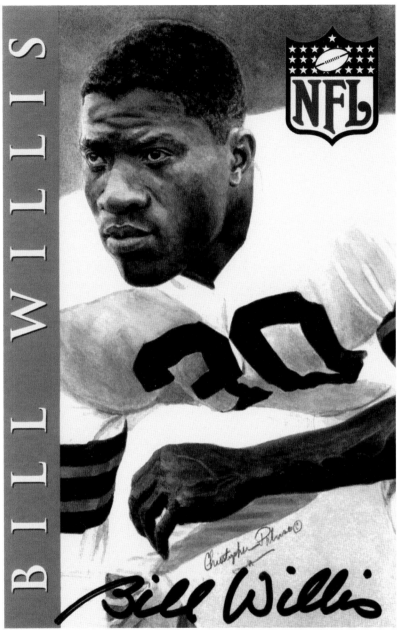

BILL WILLIS

William Karnet Willis was enshrined in the Pro Football Hall of Fame in 1977. The six-foot-two-inch, 213-pound tackle was an All-American at Ohio State University. He was drafted by the Cleveland Browns (AAFC/NFL) in 1946. A two-way player who excelled as a defensive middle guard, Willis was lightning quick. His touchdown saving tackle against the Giants preserved the Browns' 1950 NFL title drive. He was All-AAFC three years, All-NFL from 1950 to 1953, and played in three NFL Pro Bowls. Willis retired from the Browns in 1953. He was born October 5, 1921, in Columbus, Ohio. He recalls, "When I was in college, I didn't give pro football a thought. It never entered my mind. It just wasn't done at the time. Blacks were never considered."

Bill Willis was a two-way player with the Browns who excelled as a defensive middle guard.

OFFENSIVE AND DEFENSIVE LINEMEN

5

LINEBACKERS AND DEFENSIVE BACKS

The Eagle's Chuck Bednarik was the last of the NFL's 60-minute men.

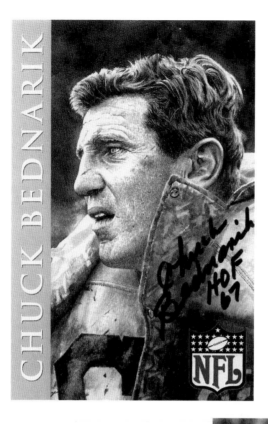

CHUCK BEDNARIK

Charles Philip Bednarik was enshrined in the Pro Football Hall of Fame in 1967. Two-time Pennsylvania All-America center/linebacker, Chuck Bednarik is known as the NFL's last iron man star. He missed only three games in his 14-season career. In the 1960 NFL title game, Bednarik played 58 minutes and made the game-saving tackle. He was All-NFL nine times, played in eight Pro Bowl games, was MVP in 1954, and was named the NFL's All-Time Center in 1969. Chuck played with the Eagles until his retirement in 1962.

Bednarik stands over the lifeless body of Frank Gifford after a tackle. He sums up the era he played in, saying, "The players of my era were not the true pioneers of football but the game became popular in the 1950s and I feel we made it what it is today." He was born May 1, 1925, in Bethlehem, Pennsylvania.

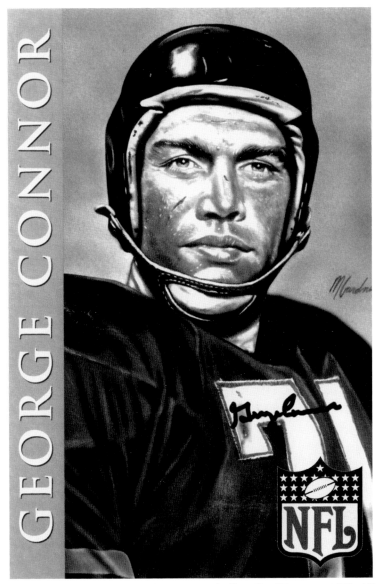

George Leo Connor was enshrined in the Pro Football Hall of Fame in 1975. All-America at both Holy Cross and Notre Dame, this six-foot-three-inch, 240-pound tackle/linebacker was the No. 1 draft pick of the New York Giants in 1946. His rights were later traded to the Boston Yanks, and in 1948 to the Chicago Bears. Connor was a two-way performer throughout his illustrious career. He was considered to be one of the first of the big, fast, and agile linebackers and was exceptional at diagnosing opponent's plays. Connor was All-NFL in three positions: offensive tackle, defensive tackle, and linebacker, and All-NFL for a total of five years. He also played in four Pro Bowl games from 1950 to 1953. Connor ended his career with the Bears in 1955. He was born January 21, 1925, in Chicago and died March 31, 2003, at age 78. He describes his play, "Any slick quarterback can fool you if you try to follow the ball but watching a few key players will lead you right to the play."

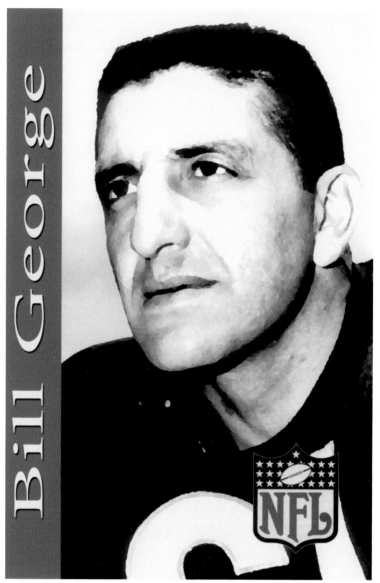

Bill George

William J. George was enshrined in the Pro Football Hall of Fame in 1974. An outstanding linebacker out of Wake Forest University, George was the Chicago Bears' No. 2 future draft choice in 1951. At six feet, two inches and 237 pounds, he was considered to be one of the first great middle linebackers. George called the Bears' defensive signals for eight years. He was All-NFL for eight years, played in eight straight Pro Bowls in 1955–1962, had a career record 18 interceptions, and recovered 19 opponents' fumbles. Bill George's career with the Chicago Bears spanned from 1952 to 1965 and ended with the Los Angeles Rams in 1966. He was born October 27, 1929, in Waynesburg, Pennsylvania, and died September 30, 1982, at age 52. He said, "Football has been very good to me. Perhaps someday we can instill that same team and football spirit that at one time we all believed in. I'm certainly proud to be a part of the Pro Football Hall of Fame. I just hope that there is no way they can take that away from me."

Robert Lee "Sam" Huff was enshrined in the Pro Football Hall of Fame in 1982. An All-America guard at West Virginia, Huff was the No. 3 draft pick of the New York Giants in 1956. At six feet, one inch and 230 pounds, Huff had 30 career interceptions, played in six NFL title games, five Pro Bowl games, was All-NFL three years, and the Redskins player-coach in 1969. His football career with the New York Giants spanned from 1956 to 1963 and with the Washington Redskins from 1964 to 1967, 1969. He was born October 4, 1934, in Morgantown, West Virginia.

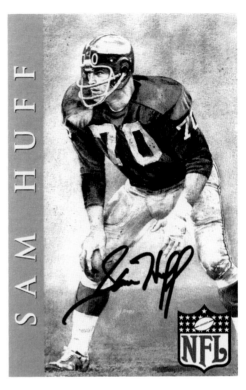

Huff was one of the league's greats when it came to playing the linebacker position. Known as a hard hitting player, Sam Huff was named the NFL's top linebacker in 1959. He recalls the end of his career: "I knew I could have continued to play. I just didn't know if I could have taken another one of Lombardi's training camps."

Ray Nitschke

Raymond Ernest Nitschke was enshrined in the Pro Football Hall of Fame in 1978. Nitschke was the No. 3 draft pick of the Green Bay Packers in 1958. A middle linebacker out of Illinois, Nitschke was fast, tough, and strong. At six feet, three inches and 235 pounds, he was a menacing defender on rushes and against the pass. He was named the NFL's All-Time Top Linebacker in 1969 and was All-NFL three years. In the 1964 Pro Bowl, Nitschke intercepted a pass for a touchdown. He had 25 career interceptions and was voted MVP in the 1962 NFL title game. His career with the Packers began in 1958 and ended in 1972. He was born December 29, 1936, in Elmwood Park, Illinois, and died March 8, 1998, at age 61.

Nitschke was a fierce competitor and was voted MVP in the 1962 NFL title game. He describes his team, "It was the character of the Packers that made us the team of the decade. We played for sixty minutes. We let it all hang out. There was no tomorrow for us. We got the adrenaline flowing and we just let it go."

Nitschke was fast, tough, strong, and a menacing defender.

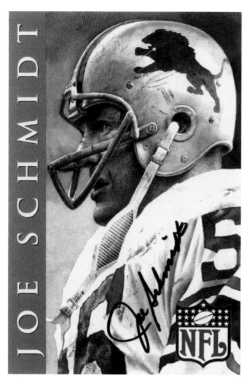

Joseph Paul Schmidt was enshrined in the Pro Football Hall of Fame in 1973. A University of Pittsburgh All-American in 1952 and the Lions' No. 7 draft pick in 1953, Schmidt mastered the new middle linebacker position that evolved in the 1950s. At six feet, 220 pounds, Schmidt was the Lion's team captain for nine years. He was elected to 10 straight Pro Bowls (1955–1964), was All-NFL 10 years, and Lions' MVP four times. He retired from Detroit in 1965. He was born January 18, 1932, in Pittsburgh.

Team captain of the Detroit Lions, Schmidt was exceptional at reading opponent's offensive plays. He described his football life, saying, "Football has been a continuous learning experience for me. It has presented many opportunities—both personally and in business—which enabled me to enhance my life."

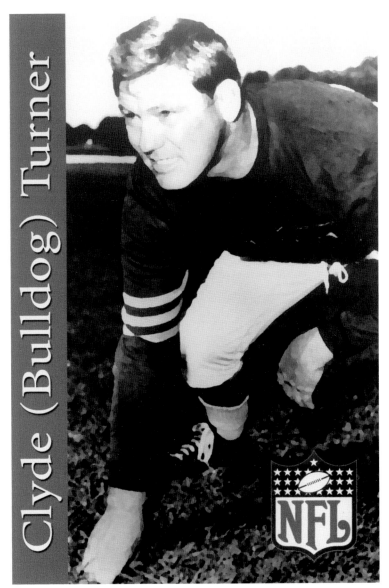

Clyde (Bulldog) Turner

Clyde Douglas Turner was enshrined in the Pro Football Hall of Fame in 1966. A Hardin-Simmons University Little All-American and Bears' No. 1 draft pick in 1940, Clyde "Bulldog" Turner became a rookie starter at age 20. At six feet, one inch and 237 pounds, this center/linebacker was a great blocker, incredible pass defender, and flawless ball snapper. He had the speed of a halfback. In 1942, he led the NFL with eight interceptions. Turner stole 17 passes in his career, was All-NFL seven times, anchored four NFL championship teams, and intercepted four passes in five NFL title games. He retired from the Bears in 1952. He was born March 10, 1919, in Plains, Texas, and died October 30, 1998, at age 79. He recalls a rule change: "I didn't like the new rules on blocking. It took away from the game. It seemed to me that there were too many people in football that didn't know football—this included the coaches, the owners and the some of the players."

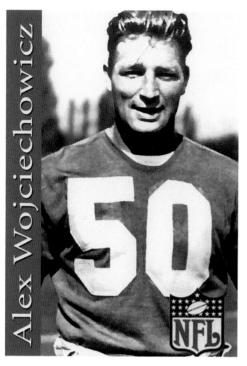

Alex Wojciechowicz

Alexander Francis Wojciechowicz was enshrined in the Pro Football Hall of Fame in 1968. Wojciechowicz was a two-time Fordham University All-America center and member of the famed Seven Blocks of Granite. At 5 feet, 11 inches and 217 pounds, he was the Lions' No. 1 draft pick in 1938 and remained with the team until 1946. He played four games in his first week as a professional. He was born August 12, 1915, in South River, New Jersey, and died July 13, 1992, at age 76.

Wojciechowicz was nicknamed "the Authentic Iron Man" and was known for his wide stance as a center. He describes a memorable moment: "My most memorable moment was when I scored a touchdown against the Packers in Green Bay. I was covering Don Hutson, an almost impossible task, when we collided. The quarterback had already let the pass go. I caught it while Hutson was still lying on the ground. I ran the ball 30 or 40 yards for a touchdown—the only one I ever scored in my thirteen years of professional football."

LINEBACKERS AND DEFENSIVE BACKS

Jack Christiansen

John Leroy "Chris" Christiansen was enshrined in the Pro Football Hall of Fame in 1970. This six-foot-one-inch, 205-pound defensive back was drafted out of Colorado State University by the Detroit Lions in 1951. He played left safety on three title teams. Christiansen was an All-NFL for six straight years (1952 to 1957) and played in five Pro Bowls. He retired from the Lions in 1958. He was born December 20, 1928, in Sublette, Kansas, and died June 29, 1986, at age 57.

As a defensive back with the Detroit Lions, Chris Christiansen is shown here with 49ers' tight end Billy Wilson. He describes how he became a defenseman: "I was picked to play defense. Back in those days they would try everybody on offense and the ones who didn't make it would play defense. When it came to technique we were on our own. Pass defense was the fun part but every team had a big running back like Steve Van Buren, Deacon Dan Towler, Tank Younger or Marion Motley who could just paralyze you."

DICK (NIGHT TRAIN) LANE

Richard Lane was enshrined in the Pro Football Hall of Fame in 1974. Dick "Night Train" Lane attended Scottsbluff-NE Junior College. In 1952, he joined the Los Angeles Rams as a free agent after serving four years in the U.S. Army. The six-foot-one-inch, 194-pound cornerback was a gambler on the gridiron who could make spectacular plays. He was considered to be a deadly open-field tackler. Lane was fast, agile, and aggressive. He set an NFL record as a rookie in 1952 with 14 interceptions. Lane was All-NFL for six years, named to seven Pro Bowls, and selected NFL All-Time Cornerback in 1969. His career interception record was 68 for a total of 1,207 yards and five touchdowns. He played with the Rams from 1952 to 1953, the Chicago Cardinals from 1954 to 1959, and with the Detroit Lions from 1960 to 1965. He was born April 16, 1928, in Austin, Texas, and died January 29, 2002, at age 73.

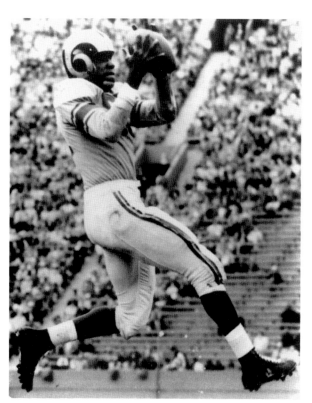

Night Train Lane set an NFL record as a rookie in 1952 with 14 interceptions. He recalls travel in those days: "We didn't fly first class, stay in fancy motels or even have Gatorade. We just played some of the best football ever."

Lane's career interception record was 68, which included five touchdowns.

LINEBACKERS AND DEFENSIVE BACKS

Robert Yale Lary Jr. was enshrined in the Pro Football Hall of Fame in 1979. Lary's career with the Detroit Lions spanned from 1952 to 1953 and from 1956 to 1964. He was the Lions' third-round pick in 1952. From 1953 to 1956, Yale served in the U.S. Army. He was a product of Texas A&M and at 5 feet, 11 inches and 185 pounds was a major contributor to three Lions' championships. As a defensive back, he played the right safety position for 11 years. Lary was also an exceptional punter and long-distance threat on kick off returns. His career statistics include 50 interceptions, 44.3 yard punting average, three NFL punting crowns, three touchdowns on punt returns, All-NFL five years, and nine Pro Bowl appearances. He was born November 24, 1930, in Fort Worth, Texas.

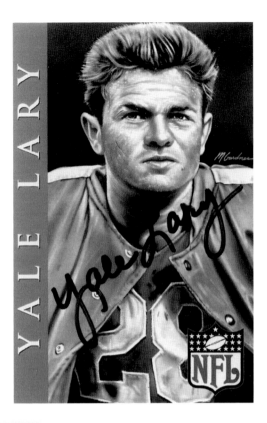

The versatile Lary played defensive back, punted, and ran back kick offs. He remembers, "One of the biggest compliments I ever got was from Jim Brown who said, 'I never knew if Lary was going to tackle me or block me.'"

Emlen Tunnell

Emlen Lewis Tunnell was enshrined in the Pro Football Hall of Fame in 1967. He attended Toledo and Iowa but signed as a free agent with the New York Giants in 1948. This six-foot-one-inch, 187-pound defensive back was known as the Giants' offense on defense. Tunnell also keyed the famed umbrella defense of the 1950s. In 1952, he gained more yards (924) on interceptions and kick returns than the NFL rushing leader of that same year. He was All-NFL six years, played in nine Pro Bowls, and was named the NFL's All-Time Safety in 1969. His career statistics include 79 interceptions for 1,292 yards and 262 punt returns for 2,217 yards. He played with the New York Giants from 1948 to 1958 and with the Green Bay Packers from 1959 to 1961. He was born March 29, 1925, in Bryn Mawr, Pennsylvania, and died July 22, 1975, at age 50. He recalls, "When Hall curator Dick McCann informed me of my election into the Hall of Fame, I asked him, whom should I thank for this? He told me, thank yourself."

LINEBACKERS AND DEFENSIVE BACKS

A monument to the great Jim Thorpe dominates the entrance lobby and the curved ramp leading to the exhibition areas at the Pro Football Hall of Fame.

DISCOVER THOUSANDS OF LOCAL HISTORY BOOKS FEATURING MILLIONS OF VINTAGE IMAGES

Arcadia Publishing, the leading local history publisher in the United States, is committed to making history accessible and meaningful through publishing books that celebrate and preserve the heritage of America's people and places.

Find more books like this at
www.arcadiapublishing.com

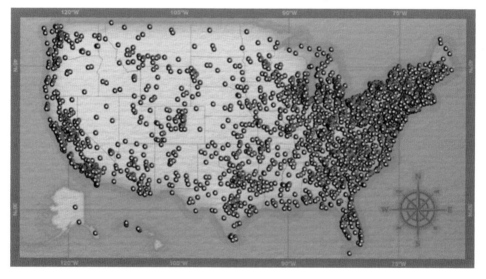

Search for your hometown history, your old
stomping grounds, and even your favorite sports team.